Jeff Toghill's Guides to
AUSTRALIAN
COASTLINE

2 WEST COAST

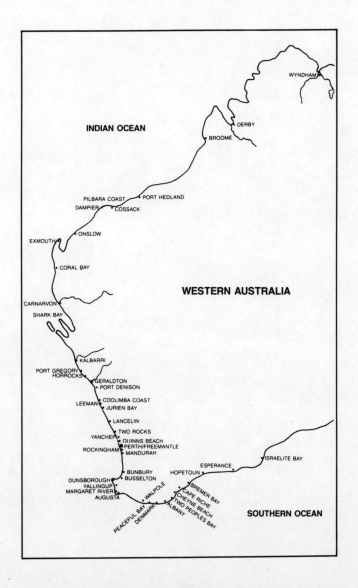

INDIAN OCEAN

WYNDHAM

DERBY

BROOME

PILBARA COAST
DAMPIER • COSSACK • PORT HEDLAND

EXMOUTH • ONSLOW

CORAL BAY

WESTERN AUSTRALIA

CARNARVON
SHARK BAY

KALBARRI
PORT GREGORY
HORROCKS
GERALDTON
PORT DENISON
COOLIMBA COAST
LEEMAN • JURIEN BAY
LANCELIN
TWO ROCKS
YANCHEP • QUINNS BEACH
PERTH/FREEMANTLE
ROCKINGHAM • MANDURAH
ISRAELITE BAY
ESPERANCE
BUNBURY
BUSSELTON
HOPETOUN
DUNSBOROUGH
YALLINGUP
MARGARET RIVER
AUGUSTA
WALPOLE
BREMER BAY
CAPE RICHE
CHEYNE BEACH
TWO PEOPLES BAY
PEACEFUL BAY
DENMARK
ALBANY
SOUTHERN OCEAN

BOOKS IN THIS SERIES
BY JEFF TOGHILL

Jeff Toghill's Guides to the Australian Coastline—1 East Coast
Jeff Toghill's Guides to the Australian Coastline—2 West Coast
Jeff Toghill's Guides to the Australian Coastline—3 South Coast (in preparation)
Trailer-Yachts
Sailboarding for Everyone

Jeff Toghill's Guides to the
AUSTRALIAN COASTLINE

2 WEST COAST

NEW AUSTRALIAN LIBRARY

First published in 1986 by
Hodder and Stoughton (Australia) Pty Limited
2 Apollo Place, Lane Cove NSW. 2066.

National Library of Australia Cataloguing-in-Publication entry
Toghill, Jeff, 1932
Jeff Toghill's Guide to the Australian Coastline 2:
West Coast.
ISBN 0 340 39726 8
1. Western Australia - Description and travel-
1976 - Guide books.I. Title. II. Title: Guide to the
Australian coastline. III. Title: West Coast.
919.41'0463

Typeset and produced by Jeff Toghill Productions.
Printed and bound in Singapore by Singapore National Printers.

CONTENTS

INTRODUCTION

There are literally thousands of superb holiday spots around the coastline of Australia. Some are small, some large, some well known, some unknown. Some are suitable for all sizes and shapes of families, some are not suited to families with very small children. Some have luxury accommodation, some have only a place to pitch a tent. Some have good fishing, some have no facilities for fishing at all. Some are ideal for all kinds of boating activities and some are suitable only for rubber duckies!

There is not much fun in driving all the way out to what looks like a promising spot, only to find that it is not at all suitable for your needs. That, for example, there is only heavy surf and no quiet water for your toddlers to swim or paddle. Or there is good offshore fishing, but nowhere to launch your boat. Or there is only caravan accommodation and you don't have a caravan!

This book resolves all such problems by providing in-depth detail of each spot along the coastline that is accessible by conventional vehicle. There is no need to take a long, often bumpy and dusty drive out from the highway to find out what a coastal spot offers, this book provides all the details, even to the condition of the access road. Fishing, boating, sailing, water-skiing, sailboarding, sunning, bushwalking, sightseeing or just browsing through historic old relics—whatever takes your fancy, you will find all the details listed in this book.

Information about the available accommodation enables you to plan and book ahead, while descriptions of the type of fishing available enable you to determine what gear to take. If you tow a caravan or trailer-yacht, you can learn in advance what the road and boat launching conditions are like and thus avoid frustrating and unnecessary journeys over roads that are too rough, or to ramps that are not suitable for your craft. If your interest lies away from the water, then this book describes the national parks in the area and any historical or other interesting features which will be worth a visit. It is a complete guide to the coastline to be studied when planning a holiday, and to be taken along for reference while enjoying that holiday.

Although the capital cities, with their associated waterways, are located on the coast they have been deliberately excluded from this book for two main reaons. Firstly, this is a holiday guide and most people head out of cities for their holiday. Secondly, there would not be room in a book of this kind to do justice to the many leisure activities available in the metropolitan areas, and also list all those available along the coast. There are numerous publications which provide details of holiday facilities in the major population centres.

A WORD OF WARNING!

Australia's coastline, while being one of the most beautiful in the world, can also be one of the most treacherous. The joy of a coastal holiday can quickly turn to tragedy if care and commonsense are left at home. Cities are not the only places where dangers are present; a snake in the bush or the undertow of a surf beach can endanger a child's life as certainly as cars on a busy road.

Awareness of the dangers and the use of commonsense in avoiding them are two prime factors in making a holiday safe and enjoyable, and preventing the tragedies which every year claim lives unnecessarily. Water activities by their very nature involve risks, but such risks can be minimised if children are kept under close supervision and adults are keenly aware of the dangers.

Nowhere are the dangers greater than at the small, isolated spots along the coastline which are often the most popular with holidaying families. The very remoteness which creates their attraction may mean no beach patrols, no shark meshing and no offshore rescue organisations. It follows that greater care must be exercised in these isolated spots than in the major holiday centres where emergency services are ready and close at hand.

Maritime nasties

The clear blue waters of the Australian coast are seductive in both appearance and temperature. But in those warm, enticing waters lurk many dangers, not least of which are dangerous fish and animals. Particularly is this the case in the tropical regions where many a happy holiday has ended in tragedy as the result of a sting or bite from a maritime 'nasty'. Awareness of the dangers and care when swimming or wading are the only ways to avoid what can at best be an excrutiatingly painful experience, and at worst can be a fatal attack.

The Box Jellyfish, a member of the Chironex family, is one of the most insidious of all beach dangers. Confined mostly to tropical waters, it is almost invisible even in clear water, yet has tentacles which, on a jellyfish as small as 8 centimetres in diameter, can kill a child, and on a Chironex of 11 centimetres diameter, can kill an adult. The sting leaves a characteristic 'whip' mark on the skin which quickly swells and causes excrutiating pain. The most effective treatment is to lie the patient on his or her back and treat the affected area with vinegar, at the same time calling urgently for trained medical assistance.

The Chironex is most prevelant in tropical waters between the months of November and March when particular care should be taken if swimming or paddling from a beach. A wise precaution is to carry with you a special pamphlet on marine stingers issued by the Queensland Government Division of Health and Information, 5 Costin Street, Fortitude Valley, Queensland 4006.

Sharks and sea snakes may be found in any coastal waters, and without doubt the best counter to either is to keep a sharp lookout for them. The summer months are the highest risk months, although in tropical and murky waters the risk is always present. As a general rule these nasties do not attack in shallow water, so staying close to the beach is far safer than swimming well offshore. However, some sharks, notably the White Pointer, and certain species of sea snakes, will attack in any depth of water, so be on guard at all times when swimming in waters which are the known haunts of these dangers.

Stonefish and stingrays can cause excrutiating pain and even death if accidentally stepped on. The best prevention is to wear shoes at all times when walking on coral reefs or sandy bottoms in estuary waters. The stonefish is so well camouflaged it is impossible to see and the stingray settles into sandy bottoms where it virtually disappears. Crocodiles are a growing danger, particularly in the rivers and estuaries of the northern coastlines. Protection from hunters has given these animals a chance to proliferate, and attacks have increased considerably in recent years. Stay out of waters known to be the haunt of this swift and vicious killer.

Surf and tide rips

You have only to stand at the edge of a decent surf to feel the undertow pulling at your feet as the wave draws back. Similar swirling currents can easily whisk swimmers away from the beach before they have time to realise what is happening. Where a beach is patrolled, the safe areas are usually marked by flags and only the foolhardy swim beyond those flags. But on isolated beaches there may be no flags and no lifeguard, yet the undertow can be just as devastating. Weak swimmers can be quickly swept from the beach and carried well out to sea.

If you happen to be caught in such a mishap, remember the golden rule—allow the current to take you. Attempting to fight it by swimming back towards the beach will mean almost certain exhaustion and the risk of drowning. Allow yourself to be carried along until the strength of the current weakens, then swim towards the nearest shore. If there are others on the beach, raise an arm to indicate that you are in difficulty, but above all keep calm and do not panic.

Bars and offshore waters

Many rivers and estuaries are affected by a bar. This is a build-up of sand or silt which creates dangerous sea conditions when the ocean swell breaks on it. Small boats putting out to sea must be very aware of the state of the bar, for more boating accidents occur on bars than anywhere else.

One of the greatest problems lies in the way in which the sea condition on a bar can change. Small boats putting out to sea for a day's fishing in offshore waters may find the bar quite moderate and easy to cross as they head out in the early morning. Yet by the time they return it may have changed into a raging, uncrossable maelstrom. Coming in from seawards means riding on the back of the waves—a

position from which it is often difficult to see the state of the bar or pick the right spot to cross.

Bars are affected by two main factors—the sea condition and the state of the tide. The normal dangers of a bar are aggravated by an outrun of tide, and the basic rule is never to cross a bar on a falling or ebbing tide. Only attempt to cross on the rising or flooding tide. The sea condition will depend on the wind and weather, and every offshore fisherman worth his salt should be aware of what the wind and weather is likely to do while he is offshore.

Bushwalking hazards

The coastal national parks are a delightful part of our coastal heritage and as such are enjoyed by thousands of vacationers each year. There are few dangers in bushwalking other than those which are obvious, and rangers located usually near the entrance to each national park will advise of any unique local problems. Snakes are always a danger and it is important to wear the right footwear when walking through the bush. Leather boots, preferably with high sides, are the only safe footgear to wear in the bush.

Other bush nasties, such as venomous spiders, are rare, but in all cases where a victim is suffering from a venomous bite, the treatment is to keep the patient as still as possible to prevent dispersing the poison through the body. The area around the bite should be bound firmly with bandages or clothing, but a tourniquet should not be used, nor should the wound be scarified.

Getting lost or running out of water are both problems that can arise when bushwalking in the larger national parks. Once again, the wisest procedure is to seek the advice of the resident ranger before setting off on your expedition.

WYNDHAM

The small town of Wyndham is perched precariously between the steep escarpment of the only high ground in the area and the mudflats of the West Arm of Cambridge Gulf. The road in to the town also treads this narrow path between the cliffs and the tidal flats, while the town itself is divided by an expanse of the same tidal flats. In short, Wyndham is almost surrounded by flat, mangrove country which is often covered by tides, and only the steep hills behind the town provide any relief from the flat monotony.

Not a particularly good site for a town, one might say. But Wyndham was born of a neccessity which precluded any selection of a handsomer site, even assuming such a site was available in the world of tidal flats which is the Cambridge Gulf shoreline. Wyndham was conceived and born in the hasty need for a port from which to ship out the gold of the dramatic Kimberley gold rush. The town was declared in 1886 and fulfilled its role well until the gold ran out. Then, like all towns associated with a gold rush, it fell into limbo. Unlike many other gold towns, however, Wyndham did not become a ghost town, for in 1919 the government established a meatworks nearby to process the meat from the Kimberley cattle stations.

Another fortuitous development gave a boost to Wyndham's fortunes with the commencement of the Ord River Scheme in 1958. This was an ambitious plan to use the waters of the Ord River to irrigate large tracts of land and produce crops which had never been planted in this region before. A huge dam was built some 40 kilometres south of the town of Kununurra and the immense area which flooded behind it was called Lake Argyle, after the historic pastoral property submerged beneath it. With nine times the volume of Sydney Harbour, Argyle

Lake is the largest body of fresh water in Australia. The homestead of Argyle Station was moved before flooding began, and preserved as a museum.

Wyndham was the nearest port to Kununurra and the Ord River region, so it became the focal point for shipping bringing in equipment and supplies, and taking out farm produce. But the crops were not as successful as planned, and Wyndham, like the Ord River Scheme, has not developed in the way its inhabitants had hoped. Still a relatively small port, Wyndham has little to offer either tourists or vacationers. The swampy shores are not conducive to swimming or boating, and the only sport of any

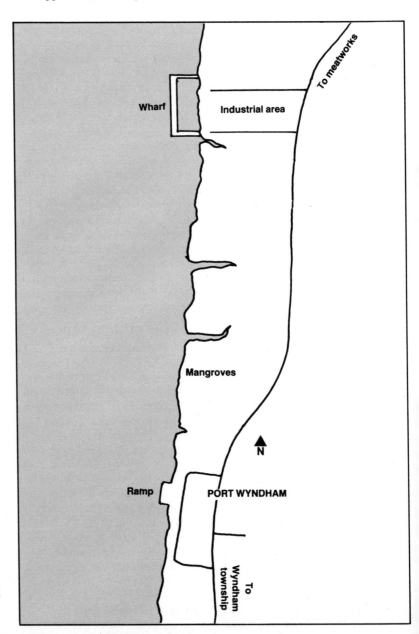

Wharf / Industrial area / To meatworks / Mangroves / N / Ramp / PORT WYNDHAM / To Wyndham township

High tidal ranges and mangroves do not make the most attractive foreshores for holidaymakers

consequence is fishing, for the succulent Barramundi thrives in these silt-laden waters.

The centre of tourist activity has shifted from Wyndham to Kununurra and its adjacent Lake Argyle. With such a wonderful expanse of water and spectacular mountain scenery, this lake has become a fine tourist attraction and major holiday centre. All kinds of boating activities take place on its placid surface. Water-skiing, sailing, sailboarding and canoeing vie with fishing for popularity. There is easy access to the water and if you do not own your own boat, there are cruises which will carry you to vantage points along the lake system. Lake Kununurra is another waterway nearby, not as extensive, but just as interesting and offering just as many water activities.

Between them, these lakes have much to offer, both scenically and in terms of water interests. Wildlife

is prolific around the shores for this is the region where a mammoth rescue project, called 'Operation Noah' was mounted to save the many unique species in the area from being wiped out by the man-made floodwaters. The rewards of that caring activity can now be reaped in the glimpses of wildlife at every point along the complex shores of Lake Argyle and, to a lesser extent, of Lake Kununurra.

Accommodation at Wyndham is limited, but at Kununurra there are a number of motels and guest houses, with no less than five caravan parks. Like Lake Argyle, Kununurra is a modern city, being built in the 1960s, and has most modern amenities for holiday families as well as transient tourists. The whole area has many features worthy of a visit, for this is Kimberley Country, and the home of some of the finest scenery in Australia's north.

By road   3227km NE of Perth
RAC Depot   Branko BP Motors, Phone 61 1305
Caravan access   Sealed road all the way
Best weather   April thru' October
Accommodation   1 hotel, 1 caravan park
Beaches   Limited. Foreshores mostly mangrove and tidal affected
Rock fishing   Poor
Beach fishing   Poor
Offshore fishing   Excellent. Launching affected by tide
Still water fishing   Excellent in estuary and river
Sailing   Good, but affected by tidal range
Sailboarding   Good, but affected by tidal range
Trailer-sailers   Limited. Launching difficult due to tide
Water skiing   Limited, affected by tide
Canoeing   Good, but affected by tide
Skindiving   Poor
Fuel and Bait   Town stores
Boat hire   None
Ramps   Good ramp, but affected by high tidal range
National Parks   Hidden Valley N P, Drysdale River N P
Interests   Lake Argyle. Kununurra

DERBY

Early explorers were not too impressed with the north and west coasts of Australia. Dutch adventurers explored and charted parts of these coastlines as early as 1622, but were dismayed at the hostile nature of the country and did not pursue their discoveries. William Dampier, one of the more persistent of the British explorers, examined Cygnet Bay, the present location of the town of Derby, in 1688. He also was unimpressed and it was almost two centuries after his exploration that the first white man settled in the district. Even then the going was tough and only a handful of rugged pioneers retained a tentative toehold in the area.

They were squatters—known as the Murray Squatting Company—and they established a base at Yeeda, 45 kilometres south of the present site of Derby. Since there was no port or even shipping facilities, they brought their cattle overland from Victoria and New South Wales. These incredible drives across the most arid country in the world were longer than the notorious Colorado and Arizona trails in America's west. The stories and legends that have been handed down from these overland drives are a colourful part of Australia's history. Similar stories surround the gold rush era, when Derby experienced its greatest boom. A giant

digger by the name of 'Russian Jack' reached the goldfields at Halls Creek after pushing a wheelbarrow loaded with his tools and possessions, overland from Victoria. It is said that he often wheeled fellow travellers who dropped by the wayside when the going got tough!

But like all gold rushes, the one which pushed Derby to prominence soon faded and the tiny port on King Sound slipped back to its original role as the outlet for the beef produced on the huge stations of the inland north. Even this role was not a really satisfactory one, for no port along Australia's coastline is less suited to handling large ships. Tidal ranges of 12 metres are com-

The north coast tides create problems for boat owners

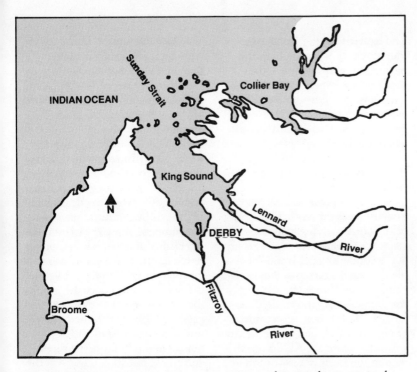

which, near Derby, are reasonably accessible. Boats can be launched over the ramp in the town and make upstream or down, while those who are without a boat can fish from the big jetties of the port. Fishing is unquestionably the most popular water activity in Derby, for swimming is inhibited by the tidal problems and the presence of maritime nasties such as sea snakes, stonefish and crocodiles.

Apart from fishing, the major tourist attraction in this northern region is the spectacular scenery of the Kimberley ranges. Located on one of the oldest land masses in the world - the Kimberley region rose out of the sea no less than 2,500 million years ago - the gorges etched into the ancient rocks create some of the most spectacular scenery in the north.

mon, and the fast currents, shifting shoals and drying banks that are associated with such phenomenal tidal movements, makes navigation a nightmare.

The protruding spit of land on which the town is situated is flat and scenically uninteresting, and is surrounded by tidal flats which dry out some distance from the shore. As a result, the town and its immediate area is not the most attractive for tourists. However, Derby is the gateway to the Kimberley region and here is some of the

most superb natural scenery in the north. In addition, the tropical waters of the Indian Ocean and the big flood rivers near the town provide excellent sea and freshwater fishing.

Indeed, the Barramundi of the Fitzroy River are legendary and amateur fishermen from the other side of the continent flock to this and other northern rivers to catch what is generally considered to be the finest table fish in Australian waters. Barramundi are mostly caught in river and estuary waters,

The tidal flats near Derby are a haven for all kinds of wildfowl

By road 2933km NE of Perth
RAC Depot Colac Service Station, Phone 91 1256, 91 1429
Caravan access Sealed road all the way
Best weather April thru' October
Accommodation 4 caravan parks, 2 hotels, 2 private hotels, 1 hotel/motel
Beaches Limited by high tidal range
Rock fishing Poor
Beach fishing Limited by high tidal range
Offshore fishing Excellent, but launching affected by high tidal range
Still water fishing Excellent in King Sound and rivers
Sailing Good, but affected by high tidal range
Sailboarding Good, but affected by high tidal range
Trailer-sailers Limited. Launching affected by high tidal range
Water skiing Good, but affected by high tidal range
Canoeing Good, but affected by high tidal range
Skindiving Poor
Fuel and Bait Town stores
Boat hire None
Ramps Good ramp in town, but affected by tide
National Parks Windjana Gorge N P, Tunnel Creek N P, Geikie Gorge N P
Interests Kimberley mountains, gorges and caves

BROOME

Long before the Dutch navigators passed along the north-west coast of Australia, and before William Dampier explored and named many of the bays and inlets, Malays visited the continent in search of dugong, turtles and pearls. They did not settle and left little to indicate their presence, so it was still an uninhabited and undeveloped coastline when the first Europeans came in 1865. They attempted to graze sheep in the district but the venture failed and farming was abandoned in favour of pearling. A community sprang up and a townsite was declared in 1883 and named after Sir Frederick Napier Broome, then governor of Western Australia.

At first the Europeans used Aboriginal divers to collect the pearl, but as experienced Asian divers arrived, the Aborigines returned to their more natural surroundings in the hinterland.

The expertise of the Japanese immigrants soon made them the most popular divers, while the industrious Chinese gradually took over most of the town's shops and stores. Broome became Australia's first truly Asian town to the point where the Japanese established their own hospital to supplement the inadeqate facility provided by the government.

By 1910 Broome had become established as the world's leading pearl centre with a population of some 5,500 and a fleet of more than 400 pearling luggers. It was inevitable that such a mixed population could not exist in such isolation without friction, and in 1920 violence broke out between ethnic groups and three men were killed in a five-day skirmish. All European men in the town were sworn in as special constables and armed with handguns, a move which did little

to reduce the tension in the town, but which eventually achieved some semblance of order.

Although the pearls were highly prized, the main trade was in shell. Mother-of-pearl was in great demand for buttons and ornaments until the introduction of plastics which created an immediate depression in the pearling industry. As one door closed, another opened, and in 1965, when the death knell of the pearling industry seemed to be tolling, a cultured pearl farm was established and the industry sprang to life again. The demand was still for shell, but this time for live shell into which to introduce the 'seed' of the cultured pearl. Nowadays, the pearling luggers work the offshore waters between April and September and Broome is the supply and communications centre of the operations.

Tourism has fast become a second major industry for this historic northern town, for in addition to the interest of the pearling, the close proximity of the beautiful Kimberley region provides added incentive for visitors to either stop-over or stay at Broome. It is a magnificent spot in which to spend the winter, far from the bleak, cold climate of the southern cities, lying only 18 degrees south of the equator, well within the tropics. It has a great deal of character, with its mixture of oriental and colonial buildings and it can still claim to be one of the most cosmopolitan of all Australian townships, with its mixture of Japanese, Chinese, Koepang, Malay and European settlers rubbing shoulders with the Aboriginal inhabitants.

Although the coastal shipping trade has declined in recent years, still many overseas vessels berth at the deepwater port which was built in 1966 to provide an outlet for the export of Kimberley meat to overseas markets. Prior to the construc-

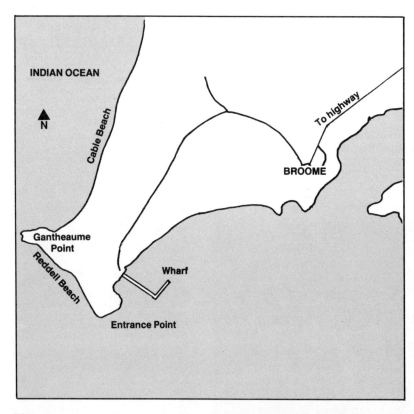

tion of this wharf, ships calling at Broome sat on the mud at low tide and were often left high and dry until the flood tide refloated them. The high tidal range still affects much of the maritime activity of the town, and luggers are usually left sitting on the mud at Streeters Jetty between high tides. Small boats can launch from the ramps at most states of the tide, but the high rise and fall creates many navigational problems, notably fast-running tidal streams, so boat owners must be aware of these dangers when heading out into the open sea.

Tourists will find a wealth of interesting features in and around the town of Broome. Apart from the countryside of the hinterland, in the immediate vicinity of the town are a number of relics of the multi-racial past of this pearling town. The Japanese Cemetery goes back to early pearling days, with headstones dating back to 1896, and an obelisk bearing testimony to the ravages of cyclones which have caused the deaths of hundreds of pearling men. An equally sombre memorial is the remains of the Dutch flying boat wrecks in

Roebuck Bay. These can be sighted at low tide—a grim reminder of World War 2 when Japanese bombers sank the flying boats—loaded with evacuated women and children—at their moorings.

Holiday fun for families comes in numerous ways in Broome. There is a magnificent white beach, extending for some 20 kilometres from near the town, which is ideal for swimming. It is called Cable Beach and is ideal for swimmers of all ages, for there is relatively low surf along this coastline. For those who prefer good waves, Riddell Beach has more to offer, while a little beach near the deepwater port is popular for swimming and picnics. Swimmers and all water-users must be aware of the dangers in tropical waters, particularly sea snakes, sharks, stonefish and, in some areas, crocodiles.

Fishing is good throughout the year but is at its best in the dry season. A good way to fish is to join organised trips to local bays and creeks, for without a four-wheel drive vehicle and local knowledge, some of the best fishing spots are inaccessible to visiting fishermen.

Pearling luggers tied up at Broome

Sailing, sailboarding, water-skiing and canoeing are all available in the waters of Roebuck Bay, although tidal problems tend to inhibit some activities. There is a ramp at the end of Robinson Street in the town, and another at Entrance Point.

By road   2213km NE of Perth
RAC Depot   See Derby
Caravan access   Sealed road all the way
Best weather   April thru' October
Accommodation   2 hotels, 2 hotel/motels, 3 caravan parks
Beaches   Cable Beach, Riddell Beach
Rock fishing   Limited
Beach fishing   Good but affected by high tidal range
Offshore fishing   Excellent
Still water fishing   Good
Sailing   Excellent
Sailboarding   Excellent
Trailer-sailers   Good, but affected by high tidal range
Water skiing   Good
Canoeing   Excellent
Skindiving   Limited
Fuel and Bait   Town stores
Boat hire   None
Ramps   Robinson St and Entrance Point
National Parks   None
Interests   Japanese cemetery. World War 2 flying boat wrecks. Dinosaur tracks

PORT HEDLAND

Unlike most ports along the northwest coast of Australia, Port Hedland was not discovered by an early Dutch or British explorer. It was, in fact, discovered by Peter Hedland, skipper of a pearling lugger who wandered into the inlet in his cutter in 1829. Pearls were the main reason for coastal settlement and in the 1870s Port Hedland was home base for some 150 pearling luggers. In later years the Marble Bar gold rush created another boom for the small port, which, when the gold and pearling declined, languished to the point where, in 1946, the population was only 150.

But Port Hedland was not about to become a ghost port, even though for some years there was every indication that this might be its fate. In the 1960s a new boom

By road 1662km N of Perth	**Sailing** Good, but affected by high tidal range
RAC Depot Combined Auto and Marine Services, Phone 73 1533, 73 2367; Meldar Industries Car Care Centre, Phone 72 2367	**Sailboarding** Good, but affected by high tidal range
Caravan access Sealed road all the way	**Trailer-sailers** Limited by high tidal range
Best weather April thru' October	**Water skiing** Good, but affected by high tidal range
Accommodation 3 hotels, 1 motel, 3 caravan parks	**Canoeing** Excellent
Beaches Limited by high tidal range	**Skindiving** Limited
Rock fishing Good from outcrops and reefs	**Fuel and Bait** Town stores
Beach fishing Limited by high tidal range	**Boat hire** None
Offshore fishing Excellent	**Ramps** Good ramp but affected by high tidal range
Still water fishing Good	**National Parks** None
	Interests Iron ore complex. Salt mining. Pretty Pool.

arrived with the discovery and mining of minerals in the inland regions, and suddenly Port Hedland was rising onto another wave crest. The iron ore from the Pilbara region, one of the world's largest mineral deposits, is railed to the terminals at Port Hedland, from where it is shipped to foundries all over the world. Huge bulk carriers up to 200,000 tonnes deadweight can berth in the port which, in the boom of the 1970s, was exporting some 40 million tonnes of ore annually.

Yet another busy industry is the

Bulk carriers such as this are a common sight in Port Hedland

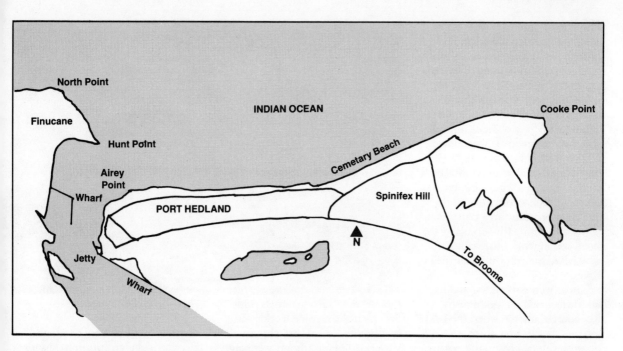

making of salt, and the boom in this product, although on a smaller scale, is proportionately as significant as the iron ore boom. Some 2 million tonnes of salt are exported each year from the Leslie Salt Company at Port Hedland. Along the North West Coastal Highway stockpiles of glistening white salt stand as conical landmarks, awaiting shipment from the port.

It follows, then, that Port Hedland is a very busy industrial port and not a holiday town in the true sense of the word. However, its ever increasing population needs leisure outlets and a number of holiday

activities are to be found in and around the town. Most prominent of these activities is fishing, for the waters of the Indian Ocean are very productive and the fishing off the coast here is considered to be some of the best in the region. The high tidal range can make fishing from the shore somewhat frustrating, and it can also affect boat fishing, but where there are fish there will always be fishermen to take them and Port Hedland is no exception.

Sailing activity is also inhibited a little by the tidal range. There is a good yacht club on the waterfront with a dredged channel providing

access to deep water in the bay. Small craft and sailboards can put off the beach near the yacht club and there is a good launching ramp near the clubhouse. Beaches are not as good as some other holiday towns across the north-west coast, but there is interesting reef fossicking available on the reefs which uncover at low tide. Take care with swimming and reef-walking on this coastline for there are many hidden dangers lurking in the beautiful coral. Shoes are essential to avoid unpleasant cuts and, more importantly, the deadly sting of the stonefish.

PILBARA COAST

The Pilbara Coast, as this region is known, needed some sort of a boom to attract settlers to its inhospitable and barren shores. The early explorers bypassed it as being of no value and even William Dampier, who explored the coast in more detail in 1699, was unenthusiastic about its prospects. It was almost 200 years after Dampier's survey that a few British settlers tentatively entered the area with their flocks of sheep. It took a gold rush, in the 1880s, to boost the area into prominence and ensure the survival of the small settlement of Roebourne which had sprung up on the Harding River.

Those were early days, and like all towns based on a gold rush, Roebourne suffered when the gold ran out. But by now there were other developments in the northwest region and since Roebourne was the major centre, it survived, albeit existing from hand to mouth until the iron ore boom of the 1960s brought new life and prosperity, not just to the town of Roebourne, but to its surrounding districts. The port of Cossack which had for so

The town beach at Dampier

long served as Roebourne's trade link with the outside world, was inadequate for anything but small vessels, so new harbours were built and near them new towns to accommodate the influx of workers in the new industry.

Workers who endure the isolation and privations of mining in outlandish regions are notoriously well paid and well cared-for. As a result, the towns in the Roebourne

district cater for every need, and pay particular attention to leisure needs. The coastal strip has become a major holiday area, with every facility for enjoyment in a climate which, except in the cyclone season, is magnificent. It follows that tourists find the area as fascinating as the locals and the Roebourne district is fast becoming on of the

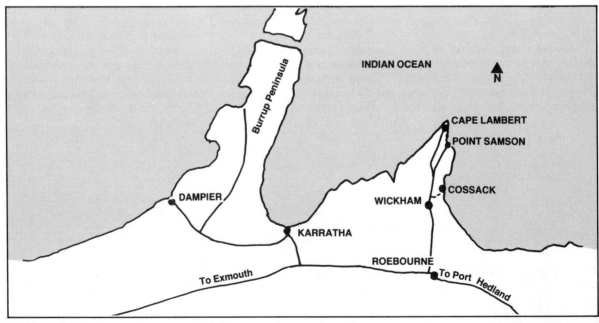

By road Approx 1600kn N of Perth
RAC Depot Karratha Shell service Station, Phone 85 1064, 85 1549;
Roebourne BP Vimech, Phone 82 1211, 87 1194
Caravan access Sealed roads to all points
Best weather April thru' October
Accommodation Roebourne, 1 hotel, 3 caravan parks; Wickham, 1 hotel/motel; Karratha, 2 hotels, 1 private hotel, 2 caravan parks
Beaches Point Samson, Honeymoon Cove, Dampier, Hampton Harbour
Rock fishing Good
Beach fishing Good, but affected by high tidal range
Offshore fishing Excellent, charter boats available
Still water fishing Excellent from jetties or rivers
Sailing Excellent
Sailboarding Excellent
Trailer-sailers Good, but launching may be affected by high tidal range
Water skiing Excellent
Canoeing Excellent
Skindiving Excellent
Fuel and Bait Town stores
Boat hire None
Ramps Good ramps at Hampton Harbour, Point Samson and Dampier
National Parks Millstream-Chichester
Interests Cossack historic buildings. Ore-loading facilities. Variety of vacation interests

major tourist centres of the north. Located right on the North West Coastal Highway, it is a long drive from southern population centres, but the road is sealed all the way and there are numerous interesting stopover spots on the way to break the long journey.

Roebourne is the oldest of the towns and has much of its history on display in the old stone buildings. The hospital, post office and jail buildings date back to the 1880s, while the Victoria Hotel is the last remaining hotel of the original five that graced the town. Its old port of Cossack was originally named Tien Tsin, after the barque that brought the first settlers in 1864. Although now a ghost town, Cossack also has interesting buildings which retain the nostalgia of those early days. The buildings are now mostly deserted and there are no shops or facilities, but Cossack is still popular with boatowners who can launch

their craft into the harbour and make out to sea. The old wharf also serves as a fishing platform and picturesque Settlers Beach is an ideal spot for a picnic.

Point Sampson took over when Cossack became obsolete as a port. It also has a disused jetty which is popular with fishermen, but it also has a very active boat harbour in which the local trawler fleet is located. This is an excellent venue for small boat activity for there is a good ramp, plenty of moorings, a slipway and a good cyclone anchorage. There is a good beach at Point Sampson, and another at nearby Honeymoon Cove. The latter is one of the most popular beaches in the area with a wide stretch of sand and reefs which uncover at low water.

The rivers in this area are alive with Barramundi and mud crabs, while access to the prolific offshore waters is easy either for private

Although Cossack is virtually a ghost town there are still many fine old buildings to be seen

boats, through the boat harbour ramp, or by charter boat. Game fishing is considered to be one of the top water sports along this coast, and charter vessels are readily available for offshore anglers who seek the big Sailfish, Marlin or Spanish Mackerel. For those who prefer to buy their fish, Samson Fisheries Store has every variety, while the local Seafood Restaurant provides the prepared product in delightful surroundings.

Wickham, which is directly inland from Cossack and Point Samson, is in direct contrast to the old towns and ports described above. It is a modern company town built to provide accommodation for workers at the nearby Cape Lambert facility. The town has a popular cinema and every type of sport, both indoor and outdoor, and it is close to Point Samson beaches and boat launching ramp, so it offers every inducement to tourists and holidaymakers. There is a hotel/motel in the town and plenty of interesting features, not least of which is the huge ore-loading wharf at Cape Lambert. Ore from inland Pannawonica is railed direct to the wharf where the largest pelletising plant in the world is located.

First of the big iron ore ports to be established on the Pilbara Coast was at Dampier. It is a modern town with massive ore-loading facilities, for it is at the wharves in Dampier that the ore from the famous Mt Tom Price and Paraburdoo mines is loaded. Railed out directly to the coast, the ore is bulk-loaded onto huge ships for export to overseas countries, principally Japan. The town is located on the foreshores of King Bay and thus has excellent facilities for all kinds of water sports. The Bay is well protected by East Intercourse Island and boasts a first-class launching ramp, a boat harbour and a yacht club. Fishing and water-skiing are the most popu-

Relics of World War 2 are still visible along the Pilbara Coast

lar sports, with sailing close behind. Although there is a beach and swimming area on the waterfront, it is not as popular nor as attractive as Honeymoon Beach and other beaches farther along the coast.

The most recent of all the towns on the Pilbara Coast is Karratha, which arose from the dry coastal plains on the shores of Nickol Bay when Dampier had outgrown its location. Since its foundation, as recently as 1968, Karratha has grown rapidly to become the largest town in the district, with a population of more than 7000, and the administrative centre of the Shire of Roebourne. In addition to the mineral boom, Karratha has grown with the boom in offshore drilling and the development of the North West Natural Gas Project. Gas collected from the Woodside platforms some 130 kms offshore is pumped to a treatment plant on the Burrup Peninsula. From here the gas will eventually flow south to all major population centres of Western Australia, while in a second project, the gas will be liquefied for shipment to overseas countries.

While Karratha is the main centre of the region and is located

on the shores of Nickol Bay, most people, both visitors and locals, prefer Cossack, Dampier or Point Sampson for their leisure activities. Karratha has an excellent shopping centre and a number of caravan parks and other accommodation, as well as a drive-in theatre, but most water activities are centred on Point Sampson, particularly the beaches in that area and the excellent boat launching ramp at the boat harbour. Dampier is also popular, especially with the sailing fraternity.

There is, then, a wide choice of activities in this busy corner of the north-west coast. There are the old historic buildings with their nostalgic reminders of the past, and there are the huge ore, salt and natural gas industries providing a total contrast with their modern structures and equipment. There is some of the finest fishing on the coast, and there are literally dozens of sporting activities including swimming, golf, sailing, bowls, diving and simply fossicking on low-tide reefs. Whatever your interest, there will be something to enjoy in the townships and ports of the Pilbara Coast.

ONSLOW

To reach Onslow you must divert from the long stretch of the North West Coast Highway that runs from Carnarvon to Roebourne. The diversion involves an 80 kilometre run out to the coast and a futher 80 kilometres back. Such a diversion is not justified for Onslow has little or nothing to offer the visitor either in terms of visual interest or in things to do. Certainly there is a harbour with a boat ramp which offers access to sea, but such accommodation as there is in the single caravan park and motel is mostly taken up by oil and gas workers engaged on offshore fields. Since the next coastal accommodation is over 300 kilometres away, a far better proposition is to give Onslow a miss and press on for Dampier or one of the Pilbara Coast towns.

The town has little or no appeal for tourists. The area which runs along the foreshore is mostly unkempt and untidy. Mangroves clutter much of the waterfront, particularly near the creek, and the surrounding countryside is dusty and uninteresting. A handful of shops, including a supermarket, caters for all needs, but beyond this, Onslow has little to offer.

In addition to the lack of accommodation and visual attractions, there is little in the way of leisure activities in Onslow. Even sports such as sailing, sailboarding and diving are neglected and the only sport of any consequence is fishing.

By road   1337km N of Perth
RAC Depot   Onslow Motors, Phone 84 6080
Caravan access   80km good dirt road from highway turnoff
Best weather   April thru' October
Accommodation   1 hotel/motel, 1 caravan park
Beaches   Limited
Rock fishing   Limited
Beach fishing   Limited
Offshore fishing   Excellent, easy access through harbour
Still water fishing   Good
Sailing   Limited
Sailboarding   Good
Trailer-sailers   Limited
Water skiing   Good
Canoeing   Good
Skindiving   Good on offshore reefs
Fuel and Bait   Town stores (Beadon Bay)
Boat hire   None
Ramps   One on town foreshores, one in harbour (creek)
National Parks   None
Interests   Oil exploration facilities

There is good fishing either from the shore or from a boat, and the offshore waters, as is the case all along this coastline, teem with giant game fish. The bay on which the town is located has two ramps, one under Beacon Point, near a disused jetty, and the other in the creek which serves as a harbour for the offshore oil rig tenders and research vessels. The entrance to this creek is shallow and mangrove encrusted.

There is a beach along the front of the town, and on the eastern side of the creek, but it is not over-attractive and, as mentioned, attracts few vacationers. Other than those engaged on business with the offshore oil drilling programme, or those visiting the Aboriginal community, it is hard to imagine why anyone would make the long detour out from the coast highway to visit Onslow.

Onslow is mainly a service port for the oil and gas industry
A typical stretch of coastline of the north-west region near Onslow

EXMOUTH

Jutting out from the north-west corner of the Australian continent, North West Cape extends closer to the continental shelf than any other promontory. This may well account for the proliferation of fish, turtles and other marine life to be found along the coast of the penin-sula. Without question, the waters of the Indian Ocean and the Exmouth Gulf are among the most productive anywhere around the continental shoreline, and it is these waters, as much as any other local factor, which is bringing the town and the Cape into prominence as a prime tourist spot.

Fishermen will go anywhere to fish, and often accompanying families must make the best of what the local scene offers, or stay at home. In Exmouth and the Cape country there is so much to see and do that it is often the families, as much as the fishermen, who are eager for holiday time to come around. Although it is a long trek north from the major towns and cities of the west, the road is sealed all the way and there are some pleasant stop-over spots en-route. Alternatively, a daily air service links Exmouth with Perth and other centres, so the distance is not a great problem.

It is hard to know quite where to start in describing the abundant interests of the North West Cape and its two centres of Learmonth and Exmouth. Apart from the clear, unpolluted water with its teeming fish, there are beaches of pure white sand that disappear into the distance and land formations that are both spectacular and beaut-iful. There are also the man-made features, such as the $600 million Harold E. Holt naval communica-tions base that commands the very tip of the land mass. Much of the Cape is a declared national park,

By road 1264 N of Perth
RAC Depot Laurie and Carol's Ampol Exmouth, Phone 49 1052
Caravan access Sealed road all the way
Best weather April thru' October
Accommodation 1 hotel/motel, 4 caravan parks
Beaches Magnificent beaches on Gulf and ocean sides of the Cape
Rock fishing Good from outcrops and reefs
Beach fishing Excellent
Offshore fishing Excellent
Still water fishing Limited
Sailing Excellent
Sailboarding Excellent
Trailer-sailers Good. Launching near Norcape Lodge
Water skiing Excellent
Canoeing Excellent
Skindiving Excellent
Fuel and Bait Town stores
Boat hire Charter fishing boats for hire
Ramps Near Norcape Lodge. Good ramp for all sizes of craft
National Parks Cape Range N P
Interests Coral fossicking. Magnificent scenery in Cape Range National Park. Harold E Holt Communications Base

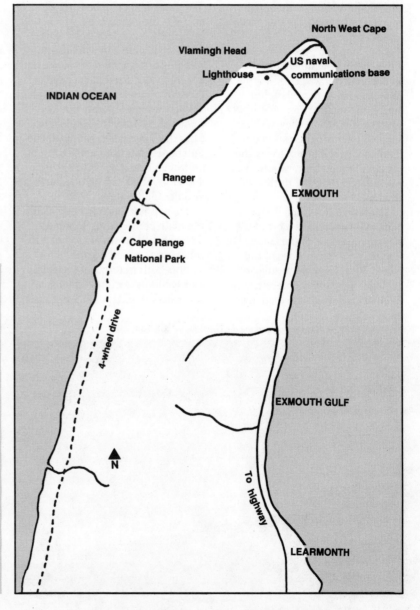

indicating the attraction that awaits visitors, whether touring or staying.

The shoreline is a major feature in any holiday area, particularly one where the average temperature between April and November is around 28 degrees Celsius. As already mentioned, the beaches are magnificent, stretching away on either side of the Cape for kilometre after kilometre, an unbroken ribbon of clean white sand. You can hire a mini moke and drive along the beaches, since walking them would be out of the question. On the way you can stop and pick up shells and other marine treasures from the reefs exposed at low tide. Turtles come ashore on these beaches during the summer, providing yet another spectacle. They are the female Greenback turtles making their way up the beach to lay their eggs in the sand from which, six weeks later, the baby turtles will emerge.

The wonderful Cape Range National Park covers most of the western coastline of the Cape. The Range is the spinal ridge of the North West Cape peninsula and provides a variety of interests from fascinating gorges which change

colour as the sun moves across the sky, to a wide range of fauna, including mountain devils, emus, scrub turkey and large numbers of kangaroo. Fossils are frequently found in the gorges and cliffs, while many of the caves in the region are decorated with Aboriginal engravings.

Access to the water for boat owners is via two main ramps, one on each side of the peninsula and a further ramp at Bundegi Beach. There is a choice of boating waters, also, for the ocean is easily reached by boats designed for open water, while small craft can work the quiet reef-protected waters. If you are not a boat owner, there is no need to miss out on the fishing, for a number of charter boats operate out of Exmouth, details are obtainable from the Tourist Officer. Sailboats, sailboards and catamarans can put off from a beach almost anywhere and enjoy their sailing on open sea or quiet Gulf waters.

There is not much at Learmonth, the main centre being Exmouth. This tidy little town of around 3000 inhabitants is well organised for visitors both in terms of shopping and accommodation. There is a supermarket and a number of stores

with take-away food outlets to cater for hungry vacationers. The Potshot Hotel/motel takes its name from the war years when American servicemen dubbed the local base 'Potshot'. Norcape Lodge is a little out of town, but close to the beach and boat ramp on the Gulf side of the peninsula. There is a caravan park in the town and another at the Cape, while camping is permitted in the Cape Range National Park.

The fishing in waters around the Cape is, as described, without peer. There are not too many rocks for rock hoppers, although they will find numerous low-tide reef outcrops from which to cast a line. But beach fishing is a must, and any sort of fishing from a boat will produce spectacular results. On the offshore reefs huge Cod are taken, together with other succulent tropical species. In the open water the Spanish Mackerel are highly prized, while Sailfish are the ultimate sport fish, one of the largest Sailfish taken in Australian waters being hooked off this coast. If fishing is high on your holiday programme, then a trip to Exmouth is a must during the winter months.

There are many other things to do in Exmouth. So many that only an extended vacation will enable you to take them all in. A visit to the Harold E Holt naval communications base is possible by arrangement, and this makes an interesting change from beaches and water. One of the 13 steel towers is the second-highest structure in the Southern Hemisphere and far higher than the Eiffel Tower in Paris. The centre is a focal point for naval vessels in the Indian and Western Pacific Oceans and its VLF transmissions are able to reach submarines well below the surface It is just one of the many interesting features of the interesting town on the north-western tip of Australia.

Fishing of every kind is available along the coast near Exmouth

CORAL BAY

Although the coastline from North West Cape southwards has some beautiful scenery and fine beaches, most of it is inaccessible by conventional vehicle and there are almost no facilities for visitors. Even the Cape Range National Park, which covers the northern

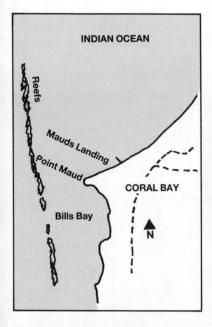

By road 1142km N of Perth
RAC Depot See Exmouth
Caravan access Short stretch of good unsealed road to highway junction
Best weather April thru' October
Accommodation 1 hotel/motel, 1 caravan park
Beaches Ningaloo Lagoon. Superb beaches along coastline
Rock fishing Good from reefs and out-crops
Beach fishing Excellent
Offshore fishing Excellent
Still water fishing Limited to lagoon waters
Sailing Excellent
Sailboarding Excellent
Trailer-sailers Good, but limited to light draft vessels
Water skiing Excellent
Canoeing Excellent
Skindiving Excellent
Fuel and Bait Local store
Boat hire See caravan park
Ramps Good constructed ramp in township
National Parks None
Interests Snorkelling. Reef fossicking

As its name denotes, Coral Bay is the ideal place to fossick for coral or shells

part of this coastline, has limited access since only an unformed road runs south of North Neds Camp, preventing the average tourist from seeing some of the most spectacular coastal features in the area. Yardie's Creek, in particular, should be accessible, for its beautiful blue water, cut off from the sea by a sand bar, lies close up under high cliffs like a miniature lagoon of the type so frequently seen along the coast of Queensland.

Coral Bay could be called Western Australia's answer to the Barrier Reef region, for it lies just within the Tropic of Capricorn and has all the popular features of the east coast of Queensland, including superb fishing and diving. It is a long way north of the population centres of the State, but it is not so far from the mining centres of the north-west, and it is probably due to their close proximity that Coral Bay is fast becoming a major tourist spot. The climate is close to perfect all year round, and the facilities, although still relatively limited, are improving rapidly.

CORAL BAY

Boating is easy at Coral Bay since the water is still with no surf, and launching is easy, even for large craft. Trailer-sailers could be launched here, and the lagoon area would be a magnificent place to sail, although only shallow-draft boats would be able to sail without the risk of running onto a coral head. It goes without saying that this is a wonderful place for small-boat sailing, with catamarans, centreboarders and sailboards able to skim across the open water without fear of dangerous sea conditions. Surfers and wave-sailers will miss out, for only in storm conditions will there be sufficient waves for them to ride. Canoes will be in their element, as will rubber duckies and other small craft so loved by children, but so often unsuited to the open beach.

Accommodation at Coral Bay is in the form of a caravan park and camping ground and there is a motel and hotel. The local store provides for most requirements, but if you have need for any but day-to-day supplies, you will need to take them in with you, for the nearest towns are Exmouth, 146 kilometres away, and Carnarvon, over 220 kilometres by road. It is a long way out to Coral Bay, but this tropical gem is well worth the trip. Make sure it is on your agenda when you head north.

The highly prized Spanish Mackerel abound in the waters off the north-west coast

CARNARVON

Although nearby Shark Bay is closely linked to one of the most significant events in Australia's history—the first authenticated European landing in 1616—the town of Carnarvon is not rich in history. Exploration was slow along this barren part of the coast and although the area was first visited by Lieutenant George Grey in 1839, it was not until 1876 that the first two settlers drove some 4000 sheep north from York to establish a claim in the Gascoyne region.

The settlers were called Brown and Monger and they can lay claim to being the white 'fathers' of the Carnarvon area, for the township began to grow in the 1880s as a direct result of their settlement. Interestingly, Brown and Monger's property was to feature in another historic event, for just over 100 years after their momentous journey from York, a NASA tracking station was erected on the site of their original holding.

Surprisingly for such a dry area, banana growing has become one of the major local industries. Since the Gascoyne River flows only in the early months of the year, water used to irrigate the bananas must be pumped from beneath the sands of the river bed. The plantations in this region are reputed to be more prolific than those of the Coffs Harbour area in northern New South Wales.

The dryness of the river also changes the geography in the vicinity of Carnarvon, for Babbage Island, on the western side of the town centre, is formed by a tidal inlet called the Fascine, since it was originally formed by the construction of a flood bulwark known as a fascine. Since the Fascine is tidal, for part of each day it is dry and Babbage Island is no longer an island, merely an extension of the mainland! It goes without saying that boating and other water activities are somewhat inhibited in these areas by the tidal conditions. However, there is plenty of water in the Boat Harbour and along the beaches to the north and south of the town.

To reach deep water a long jetty was constructed from Babbage Island in 1900. Ships berthed at this jetty brought passengers and

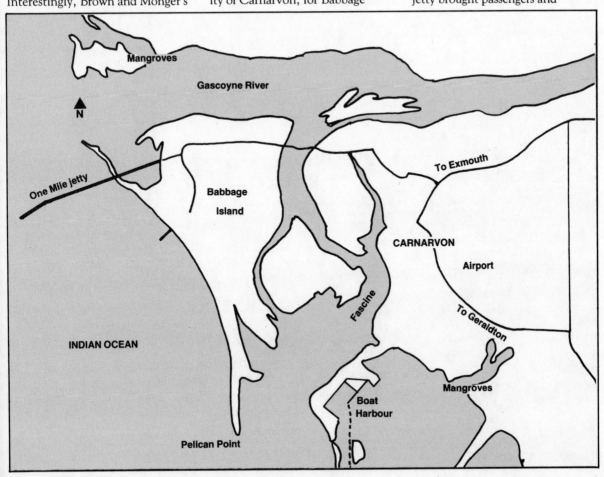

supplies to the northern town, and a tramway, complete with a puffing billy, transported them into the town centre. Although road transport took over most of the shipping trade, the jetty remains. Known as One-mile Jetty, it is around 1500 metres long and is a very popular fishing spot. Recently a pipeline was laid to dispose of offal from the nearby prawn factory at a point along the jetty, thus providing a ready-made 'burley' which attracts bigger and better fish to this popular venue.

Prawn and scallop fishing are major industries in the Carnarvon area. Prawns are taken for around 10 months of the year and processed

at factories along the shoreline. The Nor-west Seafoods factory, some 5 kilometres outside the town, was once a whaling station. As late as 1956 whaling was a prominent part of life on Shark Bay, with 6 catchers taking up to 1000 whales each year. In 1962 the whaling factory was converted to a prawn processing plant although the company was still known as Nor-west Whaling until 1984.

Holidays in Carnarvon revolve mostly around the water and the beaches. There is a popular beach near Pelican Point, on the western side of Babbage Island and beaches to the north and south along the coastline. One of the most popular of these lies just to the south of the Blowholes, some 70 kilometres to

the north of Carnarvon. A day excursion to this coast region will be rewarded with good fishing and swimming as well as the spectacular display of the blowholes, which can shoot their elaborate fountains of water some 20 metres into the air.

Similar excursions to the east of the town offer interesting non-coastal features such as the Kennedy Ranges and the fascinating Rocky Pool, which has been known to produce interesting fossils washed down from the Kennedy Ranges and caught in the pool. Closer to the town there is the 30 metre diameter 'big dish' of the OTC satellite communications system sitting atop the Brown Range, while in a building adjacent to the Tourist Bureau is a collection of

The busy harbour at Carnarvon

The coastline that faces the Indian Ocean south of Carnarvon

By road 904km N of Perth
RAC Depot North West Auto Spares
Pty Ltd, Phone 41 1159, 41 1538
Caravan access Sealed highway all
the way
Best weather All year round
Accommodation 2 motels, 2 hotels, 1
hotel/motel, 7 caravan parks
Beaches The Blowholes. Babbage
Island. Miaboolia Beach
Rock fishing None
Beach fishing Good, but little surf
Offshore fishing Excellent
Still water fishing Excellent from One
Mile jetty
Sailing Excellent
Sailboarding Excellent
Trailer-sailers Excellent, launching
easy at high tide
Water skiing Excellent
Canoeing Excellent
Skindiving Good on offshore reefs
Fuel and Bait Town stores
Boat hire None
Ramps In Boat Harbour
National Parks None
Interests Fishing and prawning fleets.
Blowholes. Kennedy Ranges. Rocky Pool

exhibits from the recently closed NASA space tracking station. This station played a large part in the successful Apollo manned flights to the moon.

Water activities begin right in the town of Carnarvon. The yacht club is on West Street, close to the Boat Harbour where yachts and fishing boats rub gunwales at their berths. The waters of Shark Bay are still, so there is little of interest for surfers or wave-sailors. But there is plenty of action in all other water sports. Sailing, sailboarding, canoeing and water-skiing are all popular with the townfolk as well as holiday visitors. Skindivers will need to move along the coast a little to find interesting reefs for the bottom is sandy and uninteresting near the estuary of the Gascoyne River.

But it is fishing which takes pride of place here. There is every kind of fishing activity possible, ranging from still-water fishing off the long jetty, to offshore charter fishing in the open sea. With Shark Bay a major source of prawns and other fish food it is hardly surprising that good catches are the norm, and few fishermen, however they go about their sport, fail to bring home a good bag full. The sandy bottom favours Whiting and Flathead while Snapper and other deep sea species are to be taken on the coastline, particularly in the vicinity of the Blowholes. Offshore fishing, whether in your own boat or in a charter craft, is the ultimate, for in the open sea here the greatly-prized Spanish Mackerel is to be found in season.

SHARK BAY

Ten years after the Dutch explorer Jansz had become the first white man to visit the coast of Australia—in the vicinty of Cape York—another Dutch navigator, Dirck Hartog, explored the west coast. Hartog landed at a spot now known as Cape Inscription on an island now known as Dirk Hartog Island. Hartog erected a post and nailed to it a pewter plate on which had been inscribed details of his ship and the discovery of the new land. This plate can be seen to this day in the Rijksmuseum in Amsterdam, while on Cape Inscription a tablet has replaced it, commemorating Hartog's achievement as well as that of explorers who followed him.

Dirk Hartog Island forms a long extension of the coastline which encloses the huge expanse of water known as Shark Bay. The area obviously fascinated the early explorers, for the names of a number of British, Dutch and French navigators are scattered across the region. The town of Denham is named after the naval surveyor who charted the Bay, while the names of Freycinet, Hamelin, Faure and Peron are liberally sprinkled across the many bays and inlets. Only the name of William Dampier, who christened the inlet Shark's Bay when he explored it in 1699, is absent.

Shark Bay is today a mixture of industry and tourism. Salt is extracted from huge pans near Useless Loop, a small community of around 250 people who produce and export around 1 million tonnes of salt each year. Gypsum is also produced in this area. Sheep have been reared in the surrounding countryside since the 1860s and wool is another prime produce of the Shark Bay area. There are a number of major pastoral stations in the Shark Bay Shire, some of which are steeped in the history of the area.

But undoubtedly fishing is the major interest, both for professionals and amateurs, for the prolific waters of Shark Bay are a legend in the world of fishing. From the small Whiting caught in tonnes around the fringes of the bays, to the fighting Spanish Mackerel so dearly sought by sport fishermen, there is a range and variety of fish to suit every angler's needs. It is the fishing as much as anything else that attracts thousands of vacationers into the area each year, and provides the basis for the newest and fastest growing industry of all—tourism.

The main centre is Denham, although the larger town of Carnarvon is still, strictly speaking, in Shark Bay. But that town is well to the north and generally considered to be independent of the Shark Bay region. It is dealt with separately in this book. A small settlement at Monkey Mia and the commercial village of Useless Loop are the only other centres of activity of any consequence around the shores of Shark Bay. Access to Useless Loop is restricted, so it can be said that vacation activity on the Bay centres around the Peron Peninsula, on which both Denham and Monkey

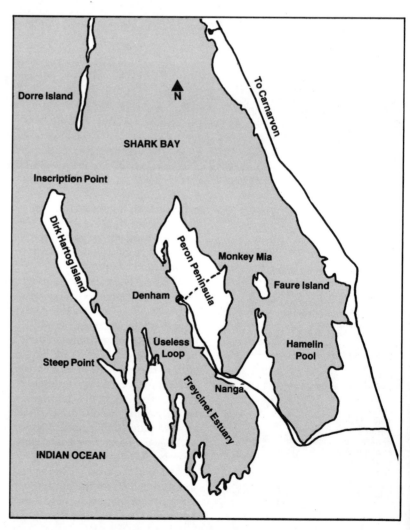

Dorre Island

N

SHARK BAY

Inscription Point

Dirk Hartog Island

To Carnarvon

Peron Peninsula

Monkey Mia

Faure Island

Denham

Useless Loop

Steep Point

Hamelin Pool

Freycinet Estuary

Nanga

INDIAN OCEAN

By road 833km N of Perth
RAC Depot Denham, Milton Harrison Engineering, Phone 48 1242
Caravan access Sealed road to Denham
Best weather All year round
Accommodation Denham, 1 hotel/motel, 3 caravan parks
Beaches Shelly Beach, Little Lagoon, Denham town beach, Monkey Mia
Rock fishing Good on outcrops and reefs
Beach fishing Excellent
Offshore fishing Excellent
Still water fishing Good from jetties and in Big Lagoon
Sailing Excellent
Sailboarding Excellent
Trailer-sailers Excellent. Launching may be difficult for large craft
Water skiing Excellent
Canoeing Excellent
Skindiving Excellent
Fuel and Bait Town stores
Boat hire Denham
Ramps Good ramp in Denham
National Parks None
Interests Shells at Shell Beach. Dolphins at Monkey Mia. Old homesteads and pioneer buildings

Feeding the dolphins at Monkey Mia

Mia are located.

Denham is a neat little town on the western shore and as such is claimed to be the westernmost town in Australia. Originally, pearling and fishing attracted many Asians into the area and at one stage the town had a mixed population of Malays, Chinese and Europeans numbering 2,500. Nowadays much of the maritime trade has declined, as has the population which now stands at around 350. It is geared up to cater for tourists and in this regard has facilities to cover almost every holiday need. The still waters of the bay are ideal for all kinds of water activities, and the foreshores of the town in summer are a riot of colour as sailboats of every kind

rig-up in preparation for a run across the Bay.

Fishing is the major sport, and except for open sea fishing farther to the north, most fishing is done in still water. There is a jetty off the town front for those who like to keep their feet on firm ground, while the tranquillity and good fishing in nearby Big Lagoon make it a popular spot with both fishermen and their families. The foreshores are mostly composed of firm sand, making boat launching easy, while the still waters of the Bay allow even small boats to sail or fish in relative safety.

Not far from the town is the settlement of Monkey Mia where a unique tourist feature has been developed. A family of dolphins have become acclimatised to the presence of human visitors and accept offerings of fish from the hand. These magnificent creatures sport and frolic in their natural environment and are a feature of

Shark Bay that should not be missed when you are in the area. Other wildlife abound in the scrub of the coastal regions. Shell Beach is one of only two known deposits in the world of a unique non-fossilised shell, and billions of these shells make an eye-hurting display of brilliant white along the shoreline.

With such a huge expanse of sheltered water, pleasant sandy foreshores and numerous interesting features, Shark Bay must have a promising future as a holiday centre. Access is easy along a good road, and there is reasonable accommodation in the form of a hotel/motel and two caravan parks in Denham, with a further caravan park at Monkey Mia. At Nanga Bay, on the road in to Denham, there is a historic cottage as well as a caravan park.

KALBARRI

There can be few spots along the Western Australian coastline more suited to tourism than Kalbarri. Indeed, the one factor that weighs against it in this regard is its considerable distance from the major population centres. It is 590 kilometres north of Perth, and 166 kilometres from the nearest centre at Geraldton. However, perhaps its isolation is its saving grace, for it is far enough removed that only visitors who have a real interest in the place make the effort to go there. It is out of range of the city weekend mobs that spoil so many coastal resorts for families and other genuine holidaymakers.

It is a long hike out to Kalbarri, for even from the highway turnoff there is still 70 kilometres to go before the clean beaches and clear blue water suddenly reveal themselves in your car windscreen. But that 70 kilometres need not be a long journey, for along the access road—which is sealed and makes for easy travelling—are a number of turnoffs into the magnificent Kalbarri National Park. The roads from these turnoffs lead to different locations along the Murchison River Gorge, one of the most superb geological spectacles on this part of the coast. No visitor should drive the length of this access road without taking at least one of the tracks leading into the gorge.

The Murchison River is, in effect, the major feature of Kalbarri township, for where the big river sweeps around the sandbanks of its estuary and heads out to sea over its bar, a still-water basin is formed. On the foreshores of this basin is the town of Kalbarri, complete with every requirement for tourists or vacationing families. Apart from superb caravan parks—one located on the banks of the Murchison River—and motels, there are numerous holiday units, restaurants, shops and entertainments. All of which guarantees that whatever your reason for visiting Kalbarri, you will be well looked after.

The basin or estuary is the prime interest for those who like their beach and water activities to be fairly quiet and modest. The fishing is good, there is an excellent ramp, there are hire boats on the foreshore, and small children will love the still, clear water that laps the sandbanks as the tide ebbs and flows. Unlike many estuaries, the Murchison is turquoise in colour and relatively shallow except in the main channel. Whether digging in the sand, splashing in the shallows or floundering in the pools, youngsters will find this a most delightful spot to release their energy. Mums and Dads will also enjoy swimming in the quiet water, while at certain times of day a gaggle of Pelicans lumber ashore to be hand fed on the grassy verge above the beach.

For those who enjoy the surge of the ocean, there are beaches galore to the south of the town, most of them top surfing beaches. Less restricted by offshore reefs, the ocean swells here create one of the biggest surf breaks along the coast— a feature which will gladden the

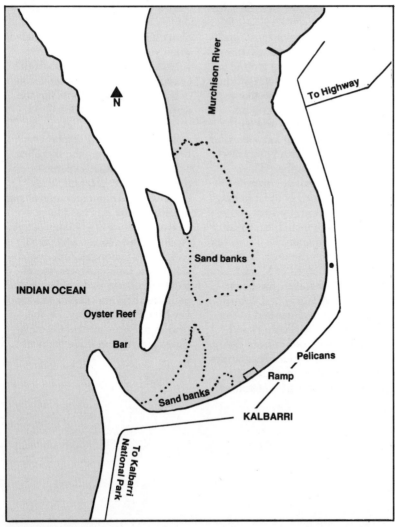

Murchison River

To Highway

N

Sand banks

INDIAN OCEAN

Oyster Reef

Bar

Pelicans

Ramp

Sand banks

KALBARRI

To Kalbarri
National Park

By Road 600km N of Perth
RAC Depot Hortons Mobil Service,
Phone 37 1173
Caravan access Sealed road all the
way
Best weather All year round
Accommodation 1 motel, 1 hotel, 5
caravan parks
Beaches Magnificent coastal surf
beaches. Still water beaches in estuary
Rock fishing Excellent
Beach fishing Excellent
Offshore fishing Excellent. Access
over moderate bar
Still water fishing Excellent
Sailing Excellent
Sailboarding Excellent
Trailer-sailers Good. Easy launching
Water skiing Excellent
Canoeing Excellent
Skindiving Excellent
Fuel and Bait Town stores
Boat hire On waterfront near ramp
Ramps Good concrete ramp into
estuary
National Parks Kalbarri N P
Interests Wonderful national park fea-
tures. Pelican feeding. Horseriding.
Murchison River Gorge

hearts of board riders, who do not get much good surf north from Perth. Beach fishermen will also enjoy this coast, while access to the prolific offshore waters is easy over a moderate bar at the harbour entrance. Take care on this bar, for although it is mostly moderate, it can, like any bar, turn savage and create real danger to small craft putting out or coming in.

The many features of the Kalbarri National Park begin with the Murchison Gorge, mentioned earlier. Others are to be found along the coastline to the south of the town. Red Cliff, one of the closest, is a spectacular headland of colourful ochres and yellows which contrast attractively with the aqua-blue of the ocean. Nearby Wittecarra Gully is connected to a number of historic events, not least of which is the marooning of two Dutch sailors in 1629, thought to be the first white men ever to set foot on the mainland of Australia. Explorer Lieutenant Grey, was wrecked near Wittecarra Gully in 1839 and set out from this spot on his historic walk to Perth which resulted in the discovery and development of many of the coastal regions.

Apart from its geological attractions, Kalbarri National Park has perhaps the finest range of wildflower species of any area north of Perth. At almost any time of year—but in particular during spring and summer—the wildflowers in this park are magnificent. Combined with the beauty of the coastal features and the Murchison Gorge, they provide a superb natural spectacle for visitors. Wildlife abounds, and apart from normal species of kangaroo, wallaby and emu that might be expected, wild goats and wild pig are often sighted in the gorge country.

Kalbarri is a must on any visitors' schedule. It is one of the highlights of a trip along the north coast, and apart from providing a fine tourist spectacle is a superb family holiday spot.

The entrance to the Murchison River at Kalbarri

PORT GREGORY

It is a long hike out to Port Gregory from Northampton, but it is well worth it just for the drive alone. The interest begins at Northampton itself, a delightful village with olde worlde charm and some magnificent old colonial architecture. It is not often you see a collection of original buildings that date back to another era such as is the case in Northampton. Gathered together around the main highway they create an atmosphere of the old pioneering days along the lines usually only found in reconstructed historic villages. But Northhampton is a thriving little settlement and all the buildings, however old, are in current use. Port Gregory itself is steeped in history, since it was once a penal settlement, and the remains of the old gaol and the governor's house are still to be seen. But first things first, and the drive out from Northampton begins with a sealed road running through undulating wheat country. This only lasts for 10 kilometres, the sealed road then gives way to a reasonably good quality gravel road and the surrounding environment also

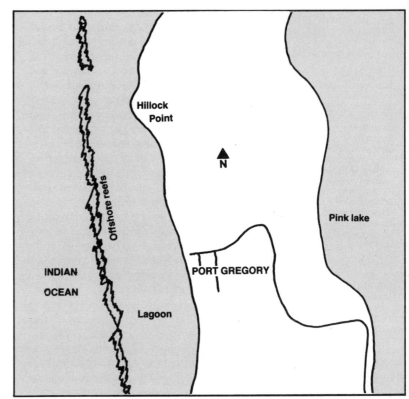

changes, the wheatfields giving way to rolling green sheep country.

This is really delightful countryside to drive through, for in many cases there are no fences and one has the feeling of wide open spaces all around. The sheep move lethargically off the road, obviously acclimatized to traffic. In the early evening or at night wildlife as well as the sheep are a hazard and care must be taken not to drive too fast. Delightful little creeks with the boughs of bushes hanging in them and waterholes surrounded by the thirsty sheep all add to an interesting and delightful drive for some 35 kilometres towards the coast.

Then the honeymoon comes to an end! The rolling green countryside is replaced by steeper hills and gullies covered with stunted bush. Rocks start to appear and there are large dust patches among the bush. But worst of all, the road starts to deteriorate, the surface

becoming badly corrugated, with some nasty patches waiting for the unwary. The road winds down through the hills and suddenly there is the old gaol and outhouses in a partial state of decay. One would hope that the authorities will preserve this fine relic before it has deteriorated too far, for already many of the buildings have been reduced to rubble.

A little farther on, behind Lynton Homestead, sitting starkly on the barren hillside looking out with sightless eyes is the governor's house—a fine piece of early settlement architecture, now almost falling into ruin. Once again, one can only hope that a priceless relic such as this will be saved, and perhaps restored before it has gone beyond repair. The old ruins look out over a wide salt lake, white and brilliant in the sunshine until the road winds around the far side, when, suddenly and spectacularly, the water turns pink!

This is not an unknown phenomenon among the salt lakes of the coast, the best known pink lake being near Penong in South Australia where salt and gypsum are mined. Perhaps it is the suddenness with which the pink appears and the stark contrast with the white salt that covers the rest of the surface of the lake that gives it such a striking appearance. At all events, it is yet another interest along a road that, albeit very rough by now, has provided a remarkable amount of interest in the 45 kilometres out from Northampton.

Port Gregory is tucked in among high sandhills right on the coast, a hot dusty little settlement, which services a small fishing fleet. The fishing fleet lies in brilliantly clear still water, locked behind a reef a few hundred metres offshore, not unlike the coral reefs of The Great Barrier Reef and Pacific Islands. It is a wonderful place for a holiday in terms of swimming, because the 'lagoon' behind the reef breaks the water down to millpond conditions, while at the far end of the beach, where the reef ends, there is a modest surf for those who like broken water. The sand dunes are high and back right up from the beach which is white sand and perfectly clean, with no sign of the seagrass which spoils many of the beaches to the south.

A sizeable jetty provides access for fishermen to their boats, and for amateurs it provides a means for dangling a line in still water. A boat launching ramp leads down onto the beach, but like most boat ramps along this coast a four-wheel drive is necessary since launching a trailer over the beach will almost certainly lead to a conventional vehicle being bogged. Vehicles are permitted to drive along the beach, but if you do so take care of swimmers and kiddies playing on the sand or a

tragedy will mar their holiday. The caravan park is dry and dusty but adequate and the small store has basic requirements for everyday needs. Since the nearest town is some 45 kilometres away, with a fair stretch of rough road to cover, you would be well advised to stock up with as many provisions as possible if staying in Port Gregory for any length of time. Water is also scarce there, but this is not uncommon in these northern areas and the camping ground should have provision for sufficient water for its customers.

Apart from the beach, there is ideal water for every kind of boating activity, from sailboarding to water-skiing. However, the area behind the reef is limited and fast boats may not operate in the swimming area. Also there is the problem of launching anything other than small craft if you only possess a conventional vehicle. However, having said that, I would emphasize that it is a beautiful bay on which to sail and

there is enormous scope for all sailing activities. Skindiving, likewise, can be enjoyed by almost anyone. Snorkelling around the rocks or the inner reef is ideal for learners, while experienced divers find more to suit them on the offshore reefs. Being only a small settlement, there are no non-water activities other than perhaps a walk over the sand dunes or around the salt lake.

As mentioned, probably the greatest feature of a visit to Port Gregory is the drive in with its attractive scenery and the ruins of the old convict gaol, to say nothing of the pink lake. However, there is a lot of beach and water fun to be had in this little spot, and it is certainly isolated if that is how you like your holidays. But take your time over the road, for it gets fairly rough at the far end and there is nothing more likely to spoil a holiday than to have a vehicle breakdown on the first day of arrival!

Remains of the convict settlement near Port Gregory

HORROCKS

Driving down into Horrocks Beach is somewhat akin to driving down into an alpine valley except that the scenario is all wrong. The high ridges and steep gullies in which Horrocks is located are giant sandhills, not lush alpine slopes. But their steepness is similar and the road twists around shoulders and winds down into the deep gullies just as it would in alpine country.

At the end of the journey, however, there is no doubt where you are, for the sparkling ocean stretches away to the horizon. It is immediately inviting, for the pale aqua-coloured water is shadowed with the dark patches of underwater reefs, creating contrasting tones with the brilliant white of the beaches. Stately fishing boats bob to the waves a few metres offshore, adding yet another dimension to this attractive scene.

Horrocks is a superb holiday spot and if a quiet, isolated holiday is your preference, then you will go a long way to better this location. As already described, it is visually pleasing and it lives up to the first

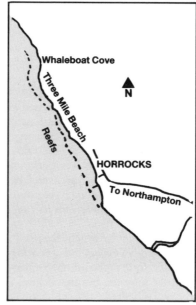

By road   576km N of Perth
RAC Depot   See Northampton, Shell Service Station, Phone 34 1106
Caravan access   Sealed road all the way
Best weather   All year round
Accommodation   1 caravan park
Beaches   Three Mile Beach, Horrocks Beach
Rock fishing   Excellent
Beach fishing   Excellent
Offshore fishing   Excellent, but launching may be difficult
Still water fishing   Good from jetty
Sailing   Excellent
Sailboarding   Excellent
Trailer-sailers   Good, but launching may be difficult
Water skiing   Good, but launching may be difficult
Canoeing   Excellent inside reef
Skindiving   Excellent
Fuel and Bait   Local store
Boat hire   None
Ramps   Over-beach only
National Parks   None
Interests   Attractive coastal scenery. Old village of Northampton

impressions by providing just about everything one could need for any kind of holiday.

The beach offers quiet swimming close in, while farther along a modest surf may provide a little fun for boardriders. But few of these north coast beaches produce much surf because they are almost all protected by the big offshore reefs running the length of the coast rather like the Great Barrier Reef on the other side of the continent. These reefs, apart from providing superb fishing, break the Indian Ocean swell so that the only waves which break on the beaches are wind waves, and they are usually much shorter and smaller than surf waves.

So swimming is ideal at Horrocks for young and old alike, and the beach is soft, white sand which makes sitting or sunbaking a pleasure. The quiet water is also ideal for sailcraft of all sizes although trailer-sailers will have difficulty launching unless they are towed by a four-wheel drive vehicle as the ramp is over the beach and conventional vehicles are liable to become bogged in the soft sand. But small

boats such as catamarans and centreboarders will have no trouble and will enjoy the good sailing conditions. Sailboards, of course, can launch almost anywhere, so they are unlikely to strike trouble.

As usual on beaches all along this coast, fishing is the primary interest. Every spot has its gaggle of professional fishing boats and on weekends and holidays, these are augmented by an invasion of amateur craft. Horrocks is no excep-

tion but is well organised for the invasion with an enormous launching ramp and plenty of parking space. There is a small jetty for small fishermen and those who prefer to cast will find plenty of activity either from the beach or the outcrops of rock. Horrocks is a long crescent of beach, so there is plenty of choice as to where and how you cast your line.

Accommodation is limited to one caravan park and holiday units, there is no hotel or motel. The store is well-equipped to cater for any needs and the delightful colonial town of Northhampton is only 20-odd kilometres away if you find the need for something extra. The waterfront is pleasantly laid out with a barbecue facility and shelter from the weather. A lookout atop the sand dunes gives a good view of the whole beach.

Horrocks is only 70 kilometres from Geraldton and an easy run out for the day if you prefer to stay in city accommodation. Make a point of taking a look around Northhampton on the way, it is a really delightful historic spot and should not be missed. I have described it in more detail under the heading of Port Gregory.

An offshore reef creates a lagoon along the length of Horrocks Beach

CORONATION BEACH

Coronation Beach lies at the end of one of the roughest roads a conventional vehicle could handle. In fact if you have the choice, take the trip in a four-wheel drive, then you can get through the soft stuff at the edges rather than staying with the bumps. The corrugations are unbelievable and a bone-shaking journey is the only way to describe the run out from the highway turnoff.

When you get there, the chances are you will not consider the trip worthwhile for although the beach is fine, there is no accommodation other than what you bring in, and no facilities, not even toilets. There is a camping ground, but it is not supervised, and there is a boat ramp of the over-beach variety. Since you are unlikely to have towed a large boat unless you have a sizeable

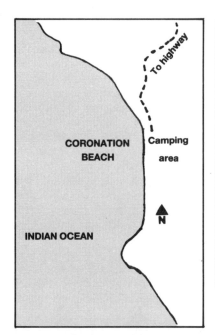

By road   447km N of Perth
RAC Depot   See Geraldton
Caravan access   Very rough access road for 10km
Best weather   All year round
Accommodation   None
Beaches   Superb coastal beaches
Rock fishing   Excellent
Beach fishing   Excellent
Offshore fishing   Excellent, but launching may be difficult
Still water fishing   None
Sailing   Excellent, open sea only
Sailboarding   Excellent
Trailer-sailers   Launching very difficult
Water skiing   Launching may be difficult
Canoeing   Good, open sea only
Skindiving   Excellent
Fuel and Bait   See Geraldton
Boat hire   None
Ramps   Over-beach only
National Parks   None
Interests   Limited

A typical stretch of coastline near Coronation Beach

'Blackboys' are said to have been named for their resemblance to natives wearing grass skirts

vehicle, the ramp will provide no problems, and there is plenty of parking space for both vehicle and trailers.

The coastline in this region is typical of much of the coastline north of Perth. Long stretches of sandy beach run in a series of shallow bays between low headlands, with a dune infrastructure of scrub-covered sandhills creating a barrier against the surge of the Indian Ocean. This surge, however, is much reduced by the offshore reefs scattered along the coast, and Coronation Beach, like its neightbours to the north and south, has only a very modest surf breaking on its foreshores.

Such a location is ideal for fishermen of all kinds, and indeed there is a small professional fishing fleet anchored just off the beach. Fishing from the beach is easy and rewarding, but the big catches are made on the offshore reefs, which means towing a boat out over the rough access road and launching over the sand. Swimming is equally enjoyable and the breakwater effect of the reefs makes the water placid and ideal for children.

It would appear that the spot is one of those access facilities allowing professional fishermen to moor their boats just off the shore and get to them by a small runabout. There are a number of these facilites at spots up and down the coast. This one, I would imagine, has been adopted by beach lovers who like to camp in the wild rather than in a camping area, and because of its close proximity to Geraldton, has built a following among sailboarders and swimmers who have four-wheel drive vehicles.

Certainly the beach is attractive, and the water superb for all kinds of water-activities. But with no facilities it is not really suited to family holidays and in any case the nightmare drive out would put a damper on Coronation Beach as a holiday spot for anyone who did not own a suitable vehicle.

GERALDTON

The latitude of Geraldton is somewhat similar to that of the Gold Coast, on the east coast of Queensland. In recent decades Surfers Paradise and the Gold Coast have become the mecca of sun lovers in the east and in just the same way Geraldton has become the 'Sun City' of the west. The two are geographically on opposite sides of the Australian continent but have much in common besides their latitudes. Both have superb beaches, both front onto a clear, unpolluted ocean, both are geared for holidaymakers.

But one thing Geraldton can claim which the Gold Coast cannot match, is an exciting and stirring history. To begin with, Dutch navigators used the Geraldton coastline to guide their ships northwards before Captain Cook was even a gleam in his father's eye. The first white man known to set foot in Australia landed here in 1629, a century and a half before Cook landed in Botany Bay. There are other stories of shipwrecks and mutiny, piracy and smuggling, for this is one of the most rugged and treacherous coasts in the world and it is steeped in maritime history.

The first white settlers to arrive were reluctant, to say the least. Cast ashore because of their part in the *Batavia* mutiny, two Dutch sailors lived with the Aboriginals somewhere along this coast. When voluntary settlers arrived, more than two centuries later, they found a harsh and arid land.

By road 424km N of Perth
RAC Depot Young Motors Pty Ltd, Phone 211 6699
Caravan access Sealed highway all the way
Best weather All year round
Accommodation 2 hotel/motels, 5 motels, 8 hotels, 3 guest houses, 5 caravan parks
Beaches Back Beach. Greys Beach. Town Beach. Coastal beaches
Rock fishing Excellent
Beach fishing Excellent
Offshore fishing Excellent
Still water fishing Good in harbour
Sailing Excellent
Sailboarding Excellent
Trailer-sailers Excellent, easy launching in harbour
Water skiing Excellent
Canoeing Excellent
Skindiving Excellent
Fuel and Bait Town stores
Boat hire Town Beach. Point Moore
Ramps Good—In harbour
National Parks None
Interests Fine old buildings in township. Abrolhos Islands flight. Various tourist interests

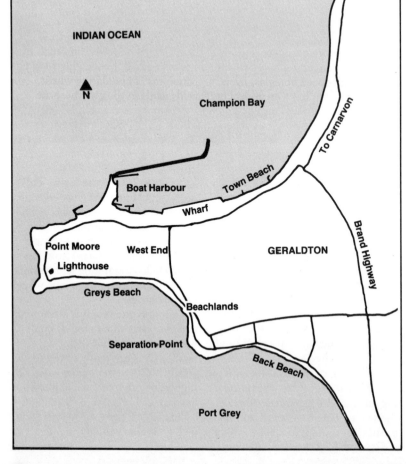

But pioneers were made of stern stuff in those days, and today rolling wheat plains along the coast bear testimony to their efforts. Sheep are also a prime agricultural product and together with wheat are the major export through the port of Geraldton.

One of the largest ports on the West Australian coast, Geraldton divides its waterfront activities between comings and goings of coastal and overseas freighters, and the busy activity of the fishing fleet which daily harvests thousands of lobsters and fish from the offshore reefs. It is an ironic twist of fate that the reef which caused so much drama and tragedy in the early days, now supports one of the major industries. It also has a bearing on another industry for tourists flock to Geraldton for the reef fishing and diving.

In terms of tourism, the city has so much to offer it is hard to know where to start. The fishing, as mentioned, takes pride of place, as do the beaches. But for casual visitors there is much to be seen in

Geraldton, for there are some wonderful old buildings located at points in and around the city. Old colonial buildings bring an air of nostalgia to a city very much preoccupied with the busy happenings of today. The old railway station particularly attracts my interest. It may not be as old as some buildings, but it is a delightful building exuding a nostalgic atmosphere of Victoriana, steam trains and wooden carriages.

By contrast there are the magic Abrolhos Islands, havens for fishermen, and steeped in the history of the early Dutch sailors who roamed along this coast. A charter flight will not reveal the Islands' history, but it will reveal the unbelievable colouring of the reef-strewn waters where the succulent lobsters are found.

One could go on *ad infinitum* about the tourst delights of Geraldton, but these will be found in the brochures published for this purpose. We are more concerned with family holidays and in this regard Geraldton again comes up trumps! There are literally miles of beautiful white sandy beaches in and around the city. The surf is only moderate, as it is all along this coast, so the beaches are ideal for small children. The water is mostly shallow and a brilliant turquoise colour which is accentuated by the different shades created by features on the sea bed. Sea grass does tend to be a problem sometimes, but there is always a patch somewhere that is not affected by sea grass, even during its worst infestation.

Moore Point is a good spot to start a holiday for apart from the beaches there are numerous items of interest here. The boat harbour must claim pride of place, for who is not fascinated by the comings and goings of fishing boats, and when the boats are unloading magnificent rock lobster, then the attraction is irresistable. You can walk right

The railway station is one of many fine old buildings in the town

onto the wharves and watch the whole process of unloading, refuelling the boats, and putting out to sea again. For those interested in boats this is a paradise for either in the harbour or up on the land there is a variety of craft ranging from the old sail-assisted lobster boats to the modern high-speed fibreglass flyers.

The port, too, has a great deal of interest with big freighters loading grain, minerals and even live sheep. Geraldton's history revolves to a great extent around its port, and there is lots to see, even if you are not allowed right up to the loading ships. Hire boats are available at

Point Moore and there is the usual take-away food and drink shops plus some roistering old sailors' pubs all in the port area.

This is just Moore Point. To the north and south there are more beaches, there is more interest. In the hinterland there is the splendid panorama of undulating wheat fields while in the city there are shops, museums, restaurants and all other requirements for an enjoyable holiday. Geraldton is a place where you could spend weeks and still never see and do everything. Perhaps that is why so many people come back time and again.

Geraldton has one of the finest harbours on the north-west coast

GREENOUGH

This is an unusual holiday spot just 10 kilometres to the south of Geraldton. It is unusual in that it is divided into two distinct areas, each being poles apart from the other. Greenough Rivermouth is a small beach settlement with all that beach settlements usually entail. Greenough valley, by contrast, is a very historic region of countryside located immediately behind the beach with a quite remarkable array of historical buildings, some restored, some in a state of decay.

Obviously not everyone who likes the beach likes historic villages, and vice versa, however, these two are so close together that it is worth treating them as one.

The river that creates an important part of Greenough Rivermouth's water fun is fed from the valley where the historic old buildings stand, looking over the sweeping countryside as they have done for decades. Just by way of introducing another contrast, there is a holiday resort located on the banks of the Greenough River somewhere between the two! This is a private resort and is not open to the general public so will not come into this guide, but is mentioned as a matter of interest for anyone who wishes to stay in the area and enjoy complete luxury.

Greenough Rivermouth is not the most attractive beach settle-

By road   478km N of Perth
RAC Depot   See Geraldton
Caravan access   Sealed road to all points
Best weather   September thru' March
Accommodation   1 caravan park (Greenough River Mouth)
Beaches   Greenough Rivermouth
Rock fishing   Good
Beach fishing   Excellent
Offshore fishing   See Dongara or Geraldton
Still water fishing   Good in river
Sailing   Good in river
Sailboarding   Good in river and off beach
Trailer-sailers   Very limited in river
Water skiing   Excellent in river
Canoeing   Excellent
Skindiving   Excellent on offshore reefs
Fuel and Bait   Local store (Greenough Rivermouth)
Boat hire   None
Ramps   Greenough Rivermouth
National Parks   None
Interests   Historic village. Historic buildings around the countryside

A typical old property in the hamlet of Greenough

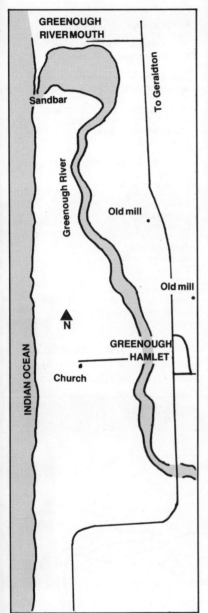

GREENOUGH
RIVER MOUTH

Sandbar

To Geraldton

Greenough River

Old mill

Old mill

N

GREENOUGH
HAMLET

INDIAN OCEAN

Church

The sandbar at Greenough Rivermouth

ment, but it has a lot to offer, it is very small, with only a few houses, a single store and a caravan park. It lies close to the surf beach and on the edge of the estuary waters of the Greenough River which is closed off by a sandbar forming part of the beach. The river is wide and, naturally, very placid, but is of little appeal for swimmers and the like since it is a muddy brown with fairly unattractive foreshores. However, the lower reaches of this river are set aside for water-skiing and include a jump and a boat ramp. Since it is unlikely to attract swimmers and is too small for any serious boating activity, this is an ideal place for water-skiers and is well used.

The beach is magnificent with a surprisingly large surf breaking along its length, although, as is the case with all the shallow beaches along this stretch of the coast, it can have trouble with infestation of seagrass which spoils its attractiveness. However, there is plenty of it and it is all clean white sand, so even with seagrass around there should be a spot you can find to enjoy the sun and the surf. The surf is not sufficiently developed to create problems for children, although it is higher than most areas along this coastline. Needless to say, beach fishing is first-class and boats can be launched by four-wheel drive across the beach, although it would probably be much easier to take them around to Geraldton close by, and put them in over an excellent concrete ramp in the sheltered harbour. Boardriding, and, to a certain extent, wavesailing may be possible here when the surf is up but I doubt if the surf will ever reach the condition that is more normal on the surf beaches of the south west of this State.

DONGARA/PORT DENISON

Most visitors to the historic little town of Dongara and its associated harbour at Port Denison, go away with impressions of a busy little fishing port. Although unquestionably fishing is major industry in Dongara and Port Denison, especially lobster fishing, there is another flourishing industry in this region which receives little publicity and is not very visible. This is the oil and gas production which supplies the city of Perth with much of its natural gas and Australia with considerable quantities of oil.

In the vicinity of the quiet little fishing port there is an oilfield with no less than 25 wells operating. The main output is natural gas, which is piped south to Perth through the 415 kilometre Wang (West Australian Natural Gas Pty Ltd) pipeline, As well as producing this gas, the Dongara field is the fourth-largest producing oilfield in Australia—after Bass Strait, Barrow Island and

Moonie—with an output of 50 kilolitres of oil a day. In the 20 years since the first discovery of commercial quantities, the Dongara field has made significant strides, and exploration drilling is still being carried on in the region.

Despite all this commercial activity, there is little sign of anything but fishing in the township itself, for it is a clean, tidy little town located at the mouth of the Irwin River, with a delightful little harbour where, to all intents and appearances, the bustling activity of trade is centred. The coastal waters here account for something like half the annual catch of 12,500 tonnes of rock lobster taken off the coast of Western Australia each year, for not only are the local reefs prolific, but not far to the northwest lie the Houtman Abrolhos Islands, where enormous catches of the succulent lobster are taken.

The little harbour of Port Deni-

By road   432km N of Perth
RAC Depot   Mobil Dongara Service Station, Phone 27 1087, 27 1019
Caravan access   Sealed road all the way
Best weather   September thru' March
Accommodation   1 motel, 1 hotel, 1 private hotel, 3 caravan parks
Beaches   Back Beach. Surf Beach. Harbour Beach. South Beach
Rock fishing   Excellent
Beach fishing   Excellent
Offshore fishing   Excellent
Still water fishing   Good in harbour
Sailing   Excellent
Sailboarding   Excellent
Trailer-sailers   Excellent, launching for craft of all sizes
Water skiing   Excellent
Canoeing   Excellent
Skindiving   Excellent
Fuel and Bait   Town stores
Boat hire   None
Ramps   Good concrete ramp in Port Denison harbour
National Parks   None
Interests   Historic buildings in town. Fishermen's memorial in harbour. Lobster fleet

son provides a haven for up to 70 boats and in the lobster season, from November to June, is a hive of

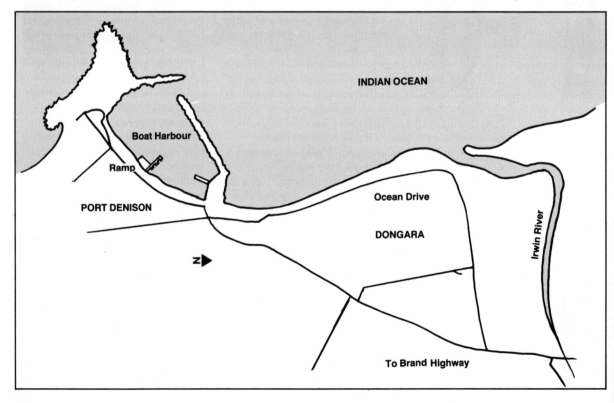

Port Denison with the historic town of Dongara in the background

activity. There is obviously a lot to see during this period, although the boats are often as active during the off-season when they fish for snapper and other species of market fish. The harbour walls are built out over a shelf of rocky reef, which itself offers good shelter for boats, and almost totally encloses a large area of sparkling clear water with a sandy bottom that creates a beautiful light turquoise-coloured basin fringed by yellow beaches.

What is good for the pro is good for the amateur and the fishing, whether it be for conventional fish or for lobster, attracts crowds of amateur fishermen each year. Some fish from the beach or the rock ledges along the coast, and the less intrepid fish the harbour waters from the breakwater walls or the jetties. But most head out to sea, for launching a boat is easy over a well-constructed concrete ramp in the harbour, and access to open sea is safe through the entrance which has no bar except when the offshore seas are really raging. When that is the case, no sensible boat owner puts to sea anyway.

Those who are not fishing-minded are also well catered for since there are magnificent beaches right at the town, and along the adjacent coastline. There can be a modest surf on some of these beaches, although it never reaches the size that boardriders would prefer. But there may be enough for body surfing and there will certainly be enough for some exciting wave-sailing. Back Beach, also called Town Beach or Seaspray Beach, is not recommended for swimming as it can produce a dangerous rip. For those who prefer still water for their swimming, the harbour beach is ideal and totally quiet. This is a perfect spot for young children, and a safe area is marked to the north of the jetty to ensure that swimmers do not come too close to boat activities.

Other water sports range from water-skiing, generally undertaken

The Fishermens' Memorial overlooks Port Denison Harbour

winds and moderate sea conditions. However, it is still open sea and normal safety precautions for sailing in open waters must be observed.

Apart from the beach and the sea, Dongara/Denison has a number of other interests, not least of which are its delightful historic buildings. From the old 'steam' flour mill which was built in 1894 to the Dongara Hotel, built in 1864, there is a wide range of historic buildings most of which are well preserved and restored, and generally still in use. The lovely old Post Office, the Courthouse, with ceilings 5.5 metres high, and some private residences all date to the 1870s, and a walk around Dongara township is a walk back into the history of this fine old country town.

Likewise, there are many interesting and scenic walks both along the coastline and into the countryside. Overlooking the harbour is an obelisk erected in 1869 as an aid to navigation. It now serves a duel purpose as a memorial to the fishermen of Port Denison who have been lost at sea and also to the brigantine *Leander* which was wrecked on nearby Leander Reef in 1853 as a result of an error in her chronometer.

You can buy fresh lobsters from the nearby waterfront stores and there are numerous shady little parks where you can picnic in style. Accommodation is in the form of a hotel/motel, a motel and four caravan parks, so the town is well organised for holidaying visitors.

Dongara/Denison is a delightful spot, and worthy of a prominent position on the holiday itinerary of anyone travelling north from Perth.

from a marked stretch on Surf Beach, through small boat sailing and sailboarding to canoeing. Trailer-sailers up to around 6-7 metres can be launched with ease on the harbour boat ramp and the offshore waters make an ideal cruising area where there is mostly good

COOLIMBA COAST

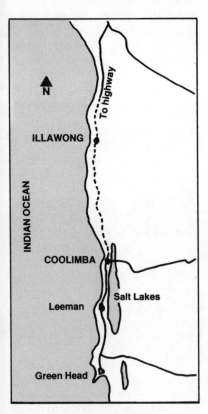

Just to the north of Leeman the coast road fizzles out into a dirt track. Although quite passable for conventional vehicles in good conditions, this track could deteriorate rapidly and cause problems in wet weather. Even in dry conditions it has many sand patches which create a trap for the unwary. This is really an area for four-wheel drives although soon the road should be pushed through as it is currently being laid from the southern end and is already constructed from the north. But in between is a road which should not be attempted by conventional vehicles unless you are prepared to take the risk of getting bogged.

There are no coastal resorts as such along this stretch of coastline north from Leeman. Where the road peters out at Coolimba, is a fishing facility consisting of a few tin shacks, a fishermen's base with diesel and other requirements, a launching ramp off the beach and a number of fishing vessels lying to their moorings. Coolimba is the first of many such access points for fishermen which have little to offer vacationers other than the beach and a boat launching ramp. Having said that, however, let me hasten to add that the beach which winds for probably fifty kilometres north from Leeman, is pleasant with clear, shallow water and little or no surf. It tends to be frequently infested with seagrass which lies rotting on the sand and does little to enhance the place as it attracts flies. When there is no seagrass the beach is quite pleasant and the shallow water ideal for family swimming, sailboarding, sailing and the like.

Each little spot has almost exactly the same configuration, with the boats moored just off the beach and facilities adjacent to the launching ramp. Fishermen use small runabout boats to get out to their larger vessels on the moorings and these are easily launched from the ramps, but as with all ramps on this coast, the sand inhibits launching trailered boats of any size without a four-wheel drive vehicle. Illawong is another such centre and Cliff Head yet another. In between there are many smaller settlements, for this coastline is a haven for fishermen, both professional and amateur. Not far offshore the big reefs lie harbouring crayfish and other underwater denizens and a very lucrative industry exists along this coastline, most of it through little outlets such as these.

From a holidaying family's point of view there is not much to offer, although access to the water is easy for small craft such as catamarans, sailboards and centreboarders. Conditions are usually reasonable in these waters, and even if a blow comes up, the developing sea is short and steep rather than large,

By road	Approx 285km N of Perth
RAC Depot	See Leeman
Caravan access	No caravan parks, rough road
Best weather	September thru' March
Accommodation	None
Beaches	Superb coastal beaches
Rock fishing	Good
Beach fishing	Excellent
Offshore fishing	Excellent, but very difficult launching
Still water fishing	None
Sailing	Good, but access difficult
Sailboarding	Excellent, but access difficult
Trailer-sailers	No facilities
Water skiing	No facilities
Canoeing	Good, but access difficult
Skindiving	Excellent, but access difficult
Fuel and Bait	See Leeman
Boat hire	None
Ramps	Over-beach launching only
National Parks	None
Interests	Long stretch of unspoiled coastline

with dangerous surf waves. In terms of 'getting away from it all', there would be few places to compare. Any number of tracks over the sandhills run off the coast road both in its sealed section and where it deteriorates into a track. Almost every one of these tracks leads to a beach, with or without fishermen's shacks and boating facilities. For those who like the beach to themselves, whether fishing or swimming, this is the place to go for you can look along the beach, even in mid summer, and not see another person.

The sandhills are covered with low vegetation typical of this type of environment and although camping is strictly not permitted there are so many old tin shacks along this stretch of the coast it would be hard to imagine officialdom coming down on a reasonable camping setup. Don't take this as a licence to camp along this beach, that is merely my observation as I saw it.

The hinterland behind these beaches is dense coastal scrub and salt lakes with little interest other than wildflowers in spring and summer and wildlife at all times of the year. There are no facilities in the way of toilets or fresh water, except at a tank called Freshwater Head, so if you plan to spend some time along this coastline, attractive though it may be, make sure you come completely equipped for every eventuality. The nearest town is Dongara to the north which has every requirement, of course, while to the south there are the little settlements of Leeman, Green Head, Jurien and Cervantes.

But for the odd fisherman's hut, the coastline near Coolimba is virtually deserted

LEEMAN

The coastal ports along the mid-north coast are so similar it is hard to find something different to set one apart from the other. Because of the prevailing bad weather winds from southerly quarters, all these harbours are snugged under the north side of headlands with the fishing boats lying at moorings and a jetty or two plus a boat ramp for trailered craft. The headlands are mostly low and composed either of scrub-covered sand hills or eroded sandstone which has been carved by the sea into some of the most grotesque shapes.

Leeman is no exception and the fishing fleet lies snugly to its moorings on the north side of the headland. Here there are two boat ramps, both very big and with a firm base down as far as the beach, at which point the sand takes over. Although the sand is fairly firm, particularly near the water's edge, I would hesitate to use a conventional vehicle for launching, especially if you have a heavy trailer. Four-wheel drive vehicles are the order of the day along this coast for although you may get your boat into the water using a conventional vehicle, getting it out could be a different matter altogether. The problem can be an embarrassing one, not solely from getting bogged, that can happen to anyone. But holding up a stream of other boats anxious to pull out and get home can create some very red faces!

Although there are fewer boats in the fishing fleet at Leeman than at most other fishing ports, it is one of the local centres for ocean rescue and is therefore well organised. Beach and rock fishing are first-class, as might be expected, but once again it is the prolific offshore reefs that bring hundreds of amateur fishermen here every year to swell the population of mainly professional fishermen. Divers also find this an excellent base from which to explore the offshore reefs in search of fish or sunken treasure.

A few small stores and a post office supply the needs of visitors and residents alike, and there is a caravan park and camping ground together with a few holiday units. For non-water activities there is the Leeman Country and Sporting Club which offers at one central location a number of activities such as golf, tennis and bowls.

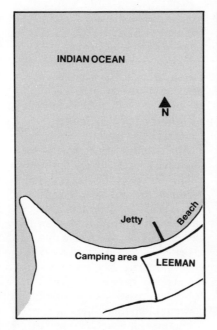

INDIAN OCEAN

N

Jetty

Beach

Camping area

LEEMAN

By road 271km N of Perth
RAC Depot BP Leeman, Phone 53 1195, 53 1027
Caravan access Good gravel road from Green Head
Best weather September thru' March
Accommodation 1 caravan park
Beaches Good coastal beaches
Rock fishing Limited
Beach fishing Excellent
Offshore fishing Excellent, but launching may be difficult
Still water fishing Good from jetties
Sailing Excellent
Sailboarding Excellent
Trailer-sailers Good, but launching may be difficult
Water skiing Good, but launching may be difficult
Canoeing Good
Skindiving Excellent
Fuel and Bait Town stores
Boat hire None
Ramps Over-beach only
National Parks None
Interests Fishing fleet

The fishing fleet at anchor in Leeman Bay

GREEN HEAD

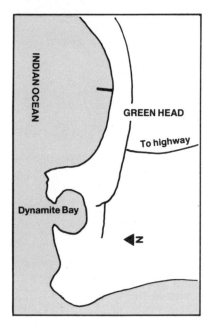

Another delightful little fishing community on the mid-north coast, Green Head has a unique little bay which has all the characteristics of a bay designed especially for tourists. In an area where beaches are measured in kilometres, this quaint little bay is measured in metres. And in an area where a rocky headland is a rarity, this beach is enclosed by two headlands forming a classic sheltered anchorage. Its name is Dynamite Bay.

Apart from its name, which must surely have interesting origins, the unique feature of this bay is its size. It is quite tiny, no more than 100 metres across, and the headland cliffs are probably no more than 4 metres high. Yet the whole thing is so perfectly formed it makes a complete 'miniature' bay, just like thousands of bays around the Australian coastline, but scaled down to Lilliputian dimensions.

However, it is not too small to enjoy, and the water is a clear aqua-colour with a white sandy crescent of beach. The water would probably not be more than 2-3 metres deep in the centre which is probably the only thing that would inhibit its use as a harbour or anchorage. The seas, already broken down by the offshore reefs, are reduced to a small break on the white sand making it a perfect playground for children. So perfect, it is a wonder that there is not a copy of it in Disneyland!

Dynamite Bay is a small indentation on the headland known as Green Head, behind which, on the northern side, is the town and harbour of the same name. There are extensive white sandy beaches on either side, so water activities do not have to be 'miniaturised' to fit into Dynamite Bay. Indeed, you would be hard pressed to sail any sort of a craft in that tiny harbour. But from the longer beaches virtually any form of water sport is possible. There is a big launching ramp in the town area, but as usual it is over sand and restricted to launch-

ing with four-wheel drive vehicles.

Smaller boats will have no trouble launching, and sailing or skiing across the still surface of the sea is a delight. Bear in mind, however, that it is open ocean, even if the swell is broken by the effect of the offshore reefs. And this is a windy stretch of coastline where a fairly steep chop can build up very quickly. The surface of the sea is still and calm for only a short time, as a rule, so take care in these waters if you are not familiar with them.

In the township of Green Head there is the usual general store and solitary caravan park. There is a public jetty which services the fishing fleet lying to their moorings in the bay, and is also useful for amateur fishermen who do not like to get their feet wet. Beach fishing is said to be good on the long beaches on either side of the town although these are also shallow and at times fouled with infestations of sea grass.

The road in to Green Head is sealed all the way from the highway, but there is an unsealed alternative from Jurien Bay. If you are travelling between these two coastal settlements, this road avoids the need to go back to the highway each time. It is gravel but in good condition and runs through interesting countryside. For the most part it is low, flat plains totally covered with very low scrub, much of which carries large patches of the well-known Blackboy. It is unusual and interesting countryside and somewhere between this road and the coast is the uniquely-named Drovers Cave National Park.

Offshore fishing is the name of the game at Green Head, as it is in all these coastal fishing ports. The professional fishermen who make up the greater part of the permanent population, are joined by literally thousands of amateur fishermen on weekends and holidays, for this

By road	331km NW of Perth
RAC Depot	See Leeman
Caravan access	Sealed road all the way
Best weather	September thru' March
Accommodation	1 caravan park
Beaches	Superb coastal beaches
Rock fishing	Excellent
Beach fishing	Excellent
Offshore fishing	Excellent, but launching may be difficult
Still water fishing	Good from jetty
Sailing	Excellent
Sailboarding	Excellent
Trailer-sailers	Good, but launching may be difficult
Water skiing	Good
Canoeing	Good
Skindiving	Excellent
Fuel and Bait	Local store
Boat hire	None
Ramps	Over-beach only
National Parks	None
Interests	Delightful coastal scenery

coast is a fisherman's paradise. When you put out to the offshore reefs, the only question is not what will you get, but how much you will get. North coast fishermen do not bring home their fish in baskets, they use garbage bins!

Dynamite Bay, a delightful 'miniature' bay near Green Head

JURIEN BAY

Although Jurien is basically a coastal fishing centre like most of the other settlements along this mid-north coast, it is also very well set-up for visiting tourists, particularly holidaying families. Like Cervantes and Green Head, Jurien is located in the lee of a headland which gives reasonable shelter to the large fishing fleet moored in the bay. I say reasonable shelter because the headlands are all fairly low and would not provide too much of a windbreak in a severe blow from the south or south east. However, the seas do not roll into these bays in the form of swell or surf since they are broken by the offshore reefs. Thus even the large fishing boats that lie here, are not too affected by strong wind conditions providing their moorings are secure.

The lack of a big swell makes the water as clear as crystal and the white sand of this coast adds to the effect so that the sea for some distance offshore is usually a light turquoise fringed by salt-white crescent beaches. These are perfect beaches for young and old although the more intrepid might like a little more surf for boardriding, wave-jumping or body surfing. Children will love the soft white sand—which gets surprisingly firm at the water's edge—and parents will relax knowing that the kids can wallow happily without some great surf wave whisking them out into deep water.

There is a small shopping centre at Jurien and a great number of non-water activities. On the approach road into the town there is a recreation camp, a bowling club, a golf course and, for the evenings, a restaurant. The water orientated activities are equally well provided for, with a large boat ramp, unfortunately probably not hard enough for a conventional-drive vehicle, particularly with a heavy trailer on behind. A four-wheel drive would be necessary. For those who prefer quiet fishing, the jetty in the corner of the bay provides an ideal venue.

The beaches are excellent for fishing as well as for swimming, and the low headland has plenty of spots for casting a line from the rocks. The ultimate fishing is, of course,

By road 266km N of Perth
RAC Depot Jurien Bay Service Station and Roadhouse, Phone 48 1053
Caravan access Sealed road all the way
Best weather September thru' March
Accommodation 1 hotel/motel, 1 caravan park
Beaches Superb coastal beaches
Rock fishing Good
Beach fishing Excellent
Offshore fishing Excellent, but launching may be difficult
Still water fishing Good from jetties
Sailing Excellent
Sailboarding Excellent
Trailer-sailers Good, but launching may be difficult
Water skiing Good, but launching may be difficult
Canoeing Good
Skindiving Excellent
Fuel and Bait Local store
Boat Hire None
Ramps Over-beach only
National Parks Drovers Cave N P
Interests Interesting hinterland scenery Local fishing fleet

North Head

Jurien Bay

Beach

N

Favourite Island

Offshore reefs

Jetties

JURIEN

To highway

Island Point

Escape Island

The fishermen's jetty is used for a variety of purposes

offshore on the numerous reefs which not only provide some of the best fishing around the Australian coast, but also act as a magnificent breakwater, reducing the savage Indian Ocean swell to a light breaking surge on most of the beaches. The same reefs provide spectacular skindiving, for this coast was detested by navigators of old, many of whom lost their ships on the offshore reefs. Relics of the ship- wrecks are constantly being found by skindivers, some quite close to the coast.

Sailing, sailboarding, skiing, canoeing; whatever your particular water sport you can do it here. Of course, that is if the wind and weather permit, for this is a windy coast and often conditions for water-skiing or canoeing deteriorate as the wind gets up during the morning. By lunchtime it is often too strong for small sailboats and can whip up a dangerous sea which may threaten small fishing boats well offshore. Care is needed in these waters as, indeed, it is in all offshore waters.

Jurien is a great spot for a holiday. There is only one caravan park but the road in is sealed and therefore access is easy. To add variety to your holiday there are numerous other little bays, beaches and fishing centres along the coast, all within an easy drive of one another. Most are described in this book, but there are a few 'shanty towns' which are best passed by without mention!

CERVANTES

Dutch navigators sailing their unwieldy ships northwards along the Western Australian coastline towards Batavia were the first to sight the area south of Cervantes which now forms the Nambung National Park. Charts dating back to 1658 carried details of the coastal features including two sand dunes around 120 metres high and clearly visible from sea. These are North and South Hummocks which are part of a unique area known as the 'Pinnacle Desert' from the thousands of limestone pinnacles, some 5 metres tall, scattered across the countryside among sand formations of differing colours and shapes. The early sailors noted the pinnacles, believing them to be the ruins of an ancient city. In fact they are calcified roots of very ancient trees which have been gradually revealed as a result of the constant coastal wind blowing away their sand covering.

The Nambung National Park and the Pinnacle Desert are two good reasons to visit the little fishing settlement of Cervantes. But there are other reasons, for there is much to do during a holiday at this spot, about half way along the coast between Perth and Geraldton. Since its main industry is fishing, mostly for the tasty offshore rock lobster, fishermen will find sport along the beaches and the occasional rock shelf, while youngsters can drop their lines off the end of one of Cervantes' jetties. Skindivers will also enjoy the prolific marine life on the offshore reefs, for the water is crystal clear along this coastline with no polluting rivers emptying their silt out into the sea. It is not unusual for divers to occasionally come across a historical maritime relic on the wide reefs, some dating back to the early Dutch navigators.

The town of Cervantes is small with accommodation available at a motel or the caravan park, and supplies from the local store. For activities off the water there is a sports complex and tours of the Pinnacle Desert run daily from the township. The beaches provide all kinds of swimming activities, from moderate surf along the coastal strips to the north and south of the town, to quieter water in the bay near the jetties. Sailing, sailboard-

By road   259km N of Perth
RAC Depot   See Cataby, BP Roadhouse, Phone 44 2010
Caravan access   Sealed road all the way
Best weather   September thru' March
Accommodation   1 motel, 1 caravan park
Beaches   Town Beach. Coastal beaches
Rock fishing   Good
Beach fishing   Excellent
Offshore fishing   Excellent, but launching may be difficult
Still water fishing   None
Sailing   Good, open sea only
Sailboarding   Excellent
Trailer-sailers · Good, but launching may be difficult
Water skiing   Good, but launching may be difficult
Canoeing   Good, open sea only
Skindiving   Excellent
Fuel and Bait   Local stores
Boat hire   Near ramp and toilets
Ramps   Over-beach only
National Parks   Nambung N P
Interests   Pinnacle Desert. Wildflowers

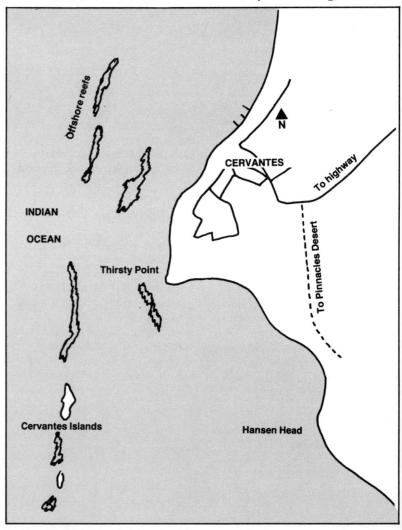

Cervantes has one of the largest fleets along this part of the coast

ing and canoeing are popular, as is water-skiing, although here again there is need of a four-wheel drive if the boat is heavy, for launching over the beach will be difficult with a conventional-drive vehicle.

There are walks along the dunes and through the low scrub of the coastal plain behind the sand hills where, in Spring and Summer, the wildflowers are a riot of colour. As one might expect in a national park, wildlife is prolific and it is often hard to drive along the road into Cervantes without squashing the slow-moving Bob Tailed Lizard who is easily seduced by the warmth of the sealed road surface. Drive with care, particularly at night, for kangaroo, wallaby and emu are around in numbers and often wander onto the road. The wildlife is one of the attractions of a visit to Cervantes and it is sad to witness, each morning, how many become road victims during the night.

Scattered islands and reefs provide the only shelter for fishing fleets along this coast.

LANCELIN

Although Lancelin is primarily a fishing centre, its close proximity to Perth and its attractive location ensure that it will also always be a popular holiday spot. It is not scenically spectacular, the town being built on a low sandy headland. It lacks the character of the high sandhills of Seabird or Guilderton and has no fine harbour like Two Rocks. Yet it must have a lot of appeal, for every year thousands of holidaymakers bypass those other centres to reach Lancelin.

Perhaps it is because there is a wider choice of water activities at this northernmost town along the coast road. There is a choice of surf beach and quieter water in the bay, although even when it is running the surf here is nothing like the 'boomers' of the south coast. Perhaps it is the greater variety of shops and accommodation. Whatever the reason, there is no doubt about Lancelin's popularity, for in summer, and even to a certain extent in winter, there are always crowds of visitors.

Lancelin is a very popular spot with sailboarders

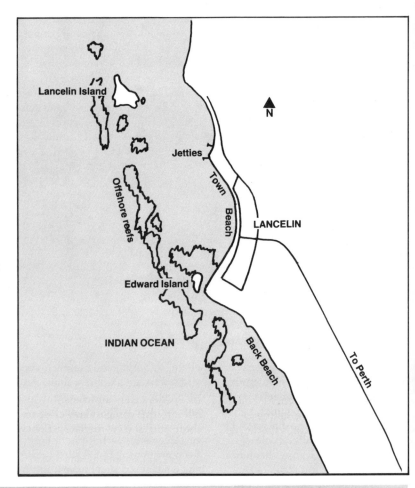

Sailboarders, in particular, like Lancelin. Even in winter the sandy point to the west of the town is alive with sailboarding activity. On a summer weekend they are as thick as flies and the water sparkles with all the colours of the rainbow as the pretty sails flip and bob across the waves. Other forms of sailing are popular too, and since you can tow a reasonably-sized trailer out over the point almost to the water's edge, sailing is a lot easier than at other beaches where you have to drag the boat over miles of sand. If you don't take your own boat, there are hire-boats available in the town.

Swimming is good because there is a choice of beaches. Young children can swim happily off the town front while those who prefer a bit of action can check out the surf on the southern side of the point. Don't get too excited about the surf, however, for it never gets up to any size on these beaches. There will probably not be sufficient for board-riding although wave-sailing should be fun, especially for the less experienced. Much depends on the direction and strength of the wind, of course, but with beaches on opposite sides of the point, at least there is always a choice.

Fishing is first-rate in Lancelin, as witness the large professional fishing fleet. There are plenty of ramps although they all suffer from the common complaint of this coastline; if you only have a conventional-drive vehicle you may have trouble launching over the sand. Many boats are launched with normal vehicles, but there is always that risk of getting bogged, particularly when retrieving a heavy boat, such as a trailer-sailer or offshore fishing boat. Four-wheel drives are the thing for over-beach launching and they are very common among boat owners in Western Australia.

If you can launch a boat then there is fishing galore in the waters offshore. The reefs are scattered across the sandy bottom from close inshore to the major barrier reef well out. All are productive in terms of fish and lobsters, and getting out to them does not take long. But remember that this is a windy coast and rarely a day goes by without a stiff breeze getting up. This can whip up a nasty sea which could be dangerous for small boats or inexperienced boatowners. If you fall into this category stay close to shore until you get more experience, and head for home before the wind becomes too stong.

Families will enjoy Lancelin, for other than the beaches there is quite a lot of entertainment for the youngsters. There is an amusement park with mini-golf and trampolines, while in the pleasant parks along the foreshores there are

By road	125km N of Perth
RAC Depot	Lancelin Engineering Supplies, Phone 78 1179, 78 1080
Caravan access	Sealed road all the way
Best weather	October thru' March
Accommodation	1 hotel, 2 caravan parks
Beaches	Fine coastal beaches
Rock fishing	Limited
Beach fishing	Excellent
Offshore fishing	Excellent, but launching may be difficult
Still water fishing	Good from jetties
Sailing	Excellent
Sailboarding	Excellent
Trailer-sailers	Good, but launching may be difficult
Water skiing	Good, but launching may be difficult
Canoeing	Good, open sea only
Skindiving	Excellent
Fuel and Bait	Town stores
Boat hire	Along waterfront
Ramps	Over-beach only
National Parks	None
Interests	Bowls. Golf. Tennis

numerous play areas. Adults, too, can amuse themselves with bowls, tennis and golf, and there is a recreation centre on the way into the town. Two caravan parks, two hotels, one motel and lots of holiday units take care of the accommodation, while there are plenty of shops and stores for the needs of everyday living.

Small wonder that Lancelin is so popular. An easy drive from Perth, it falls within the scope of a weekend outing, and from a sightseeing point of view is part of a delightful scenic drive covering the coastal resorts from Perth northwards.

LEDGE POINT

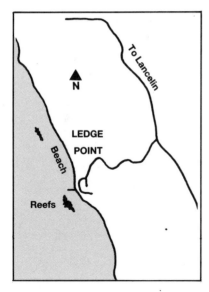

Describe Ledge Point and you are describing any one of a dozen different ports along this region of the Western Australian coastline. Seabird, Lancelin, Jurien, Cervantes, are but a few. They are all so similar that to describe one is to describe them all. Each has its small fishing fleet anchored in seemingly exposed waters, its jetty or jetties which service the boats and its ramp or ramps which invariably consist purely of access to the beach. Each has its small community made up mostly of fishermen and their families, but augmented during the summer months by dozens of tourists. Each has its local store and each has its caravan park.

Ledge Point falls precisely into the mould, for although it is only 120 kilometres from Perth, it is a quiet, unpretentious little fishing settlement with its fleet of lobster and fishing boats lying to anchor in the exposed bay unruffled by the traumas of the world. Although seemingly at the mercy of the threatening Indian Ocean to the west, the fishing fleet lies comfortably in its haven, sheltered from the prevailing south-westerly winds by a low headland, and from the turmoil of the sea by the extensive offshore reefs. These reefs provide a two-fold blessing to the small fishing ports along this coast, acting as a breakwater to reduce the big ocean swells to mere ripples, and creating a perfect environment for the succulent lobster on which is based much of the coastal fishing industry.

The settlement which has sprung up around the bay consists mostly of fishermens' cottages, supplemented by a few holiday and retirement homes. Although fishing is the main interest at Ledge Point, holidaying families find the beaches and the clear, calm water ideal for summer vacations. During the peak season, the population of the small community is swelled considerably by visiting tourists and holidaymakers. Since the only available accommodation is in the solitary caravan park, this is very well patronised between November and March.

A typical coastal scene near the tiny port of Ledge Point

The offshore reefs along this coastline create fine breakwaters for moored fishing boats

Again like almost all other fishing ports along this coastline, Ledge Point has a boat launching ramp which is limited mostly to four-wheel drive vehicles by virtue of the fact that launching must be carried out across the beach. While it is always possible to get a boat into the water with a conventional vehicle, trying to get it out again across the soft sand of the beach can be a problem. Getting traction on the beach is difficult without four-wheel drive and many a boat owner has suffered the indignity of not only having to call for assistance to get his boat out of the water, but also to get his car out of the sand!

Small craft such as roof-topped boats, sailing dinghies and catamarans will have no trouble since they can be easily manhandled across the beach without the need for a trailer. But fishing boats of any size—and boats that fish the offshore waters need to be of reasonable size—and larger sailboats such as trailer-sailers will find launching difficult without the services of a four-wheel drive

vehicle. Sailboards, of course, require no effort to get them into the water, and for this reason the smaller craft as well as sailboards are popular at Ledge Point.

Apart from offshore fishing, which follows the pattern of the other coastal ports and provides excellent sport either near the coast or on the distant reefs, fishing from the shore is also good, whether it be from the beach, the rocky outcrops or the jetty. Skindiving is superb in the clear offshore waters and many a fine relic has been recovered from the reefs which claimed numerous shipwrecks in the days before the waters were charted. However, skindiving on the offshore reefs means a reasonable-sized boat to carry out crew and gear, and this in turn means a four-wheel drive vehicle to ensure easy launching across the beach.

There is much to recommend Ledge Point as a spot for a holiday stay providing you find your interests in the open air and water of the coastal scene. But if you like

variety in your holiday activities, or if you prefer more aesthetic features, then you will need to head inland or to a different district, for the settlements all along this stretch of the coastline are, as described, like peas in a pod. Ledge Point is just one of those delightful peas in the mid-north coast pod!

By road 122km N of Perth
RAC Depot See Lancelin
Caravan access Sealed road all the way
Best weather October thru' March
Accommodation 1 caravan park
Beaches Good coastal beaches
Rock fishing Good
Beach fishing Excellent
Offshore fishing Excellent, but launching may be difficult
Still water fishing None
Sailing Good, open sea only
Sailboarding Excellent
Trailer-sailers Good, but launching may be difficult
Water skiing Good, but launching may be difficult
Canoeing Good, open sea only
Skindiving Excellent on offshore reefs
Fuel and Bait Local store
Boat hire None
Ramps Over-beach only
National Parks Moore River N P
Interests Fishing fleet

GUILDERTON

Where the Moore River terminates, it swells out into a sizeable inlet. Held back from running out to sea by a sand bar across its mouth, it spreads out under the brow of the high sandhills and forms a moderate-sized lake. Around this lake-like inlet is the village of Guilderton, a small vacation spot along the seemingly never-ending coastal beaches north of Perth.

It differs from most other resorts along the coast in that it is not primarily a fishing village. Of course you can catch fish if that is your sport, but Guilderton is not the best fishing spot. The fleet of offshore boats which is a feature of almost every other coastal spot, is notably missing here. It would seem that Guilderton is going to be different to the others and concentrate on holiday vacations instead of fishing boats.

As such, it does a very good job. The waters of the inlet, being fresh are not the best colour, but they are still and fairly deep so they are ideal for small boat sailing, and they have pleasant sandy fringes, especially near the bar, so that young families

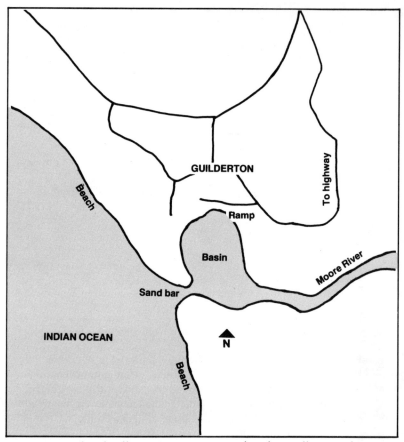

can enjoy sand and still water. There is a launching ramp near the car park, and a delightful foreshore reserve with barbecue facilities and toilets all close to hand.

Catamarans, centreboarders and sailboards are well-suited to this stretch of quiet water, as are canoes which can explore along the Moore River between the high-sided sand dunes. I am not sure if there are any fish in the inlet, but young hopefuls will probably try their luck anyway. All these activities can be undertaken in pleasant surroundings, well-sheltered from the blustery sea breeze. The store is adjacent to the car park area, and the pleasantly located caravan park is nearby.

For those with more adventurous things on their minds, such as surfing, wave-sailing or beach fishing, and for those who prefer an

ocean beach to still water, there is a superb beach just across the sand bar. The surf does not get very big here, but there are waves, even if they may be a bit tame for boardriders. There are also fish if you are good at beach fishing, for the whole of this coastal stretch is renowned for its beach fishing. There are very few rocks, so rock-hoppers will need to go farther afield.

The store takes care of all daily needs, and the shopping centre at Lancelin is not too far away if you need something extra. Guilderton is on a sealed road only six kilometres in from the coast highway. On the way in there are some interesting geological structures not unlike the 'Pinnacles' at Cervantes, farther along the coast. Other interests include a country club, a tennis club and a bowling green, all

By road 91km N of Perth
RAC Depot See Lancelin or Yanchep
Caravan access Sealed road all the way
Best weather October thru' March
Accommodation Guilderton, 1 caravan park; Seabird, 1 caravan park
Beaches Good coastal beaches
Rock fishing Limited
Beach fishing Excellent
Offshore fishing Excellent, but launching may be difficult
Still water fishing Fair in Moore River
Sailing Excellent
Sailboarding Excellent
Trailer-sailers Limited. Over-beach launching at Seabird only
Water skiing Limited
Canoeing Excellent in Moore River
Skindiving Excellent on offshore reefs
Fuel and Bait Guilderton store
Boat hire None
Ramps Over-beach at Seabird. Into river at Guilderton
National Parks Moore River N P
Interests Fishing fleet. Attractive coastal scenery

of which make the settlement a well-organised holiday centre.

Nearby is another settlement with the delightful name of Seabird. I mention it here because it would almost seem specifically designed to complement Guilderton. Where that town has little to offer in the way of professional fishing activities, Seabird has nothing else. The entire village, set high over the dunes, consists of a fishing community. And just as Guilderton is an ideal holiday centre, Seabird has no holiday facilities other than its beach. Rather like Jack Spratt and his wife, these two coastal settlements cover the needs of everyone, albeit in their own way.

Seabird has a good sea launching ramp although it is an over-beach ramp, and a tidy fleet of professional fishing boats bob at their moorings a few hundred metres offshore. But it has no caravan park. Since both villages are close together and both about six kilometres in from the coast road, it would make sense to visit them both.

The basin of the Moore River provides a quiet foreshore inside the bar

TWO ROCKS

The unspoiled sandy coast of Western Australia with its endless beaches, strong prevailing winds and treacherous offshore waters, would seem an unlikely place to stage the most prestigious yachting event in the world. Yet this is where the successful Australian challenge for the coveted America's Cup first began.

The ambitious plans of a few West Australian yachtsmen which grew to achieve an international yachting triumph were first mooted in a tiny beach resort some 50 kilometres to the northof Perth. The beach resort was almost non-existent at the time and was known as Two Rocks or Wreck Point. Business magnate Alan Bond was not satisfied with Fremantle as a base to establish a challenge for the America's Cup, so he investigated the nearby coastline and settled on

Two Rocks as the spot.

The unheard of village sprang to local, then national and finally international prominence as the Bond challenge caught the public's imagination. As the task force grew, so did the little boat harbour, to the point where it became a major centre for yachts, fishing boats and small craft using the coastal waters. The success of Bond's venture is now recorded in

yachting history. The wisdom of his choice of Two Rocks is confirmed, for the harbour is now a major boating facility and caters for every type of leisure craft from cruising yachts to small fishing boats.

With the fine entrepreneurial flare that has made him one of Australia's leading businessmen, Alan Bond moved beyond the needs for his America's Cup challenge by establishing a complete

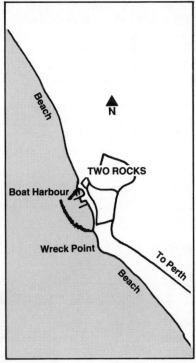

holiday facility at Two Rocks. His land development is now the holiday town of Yanchep Sun City. Here there is a superbly sited tavern overlooking the boat harbour where you can enjoy a relaxing drink while not only contemplating the place 'where it all began', but also taking in the spectacular view of the coastline and the open sea. An easy run from the city of Perth, this is a spot no visitor should miss.

For families and those who would stay longer, there are numerous delights, not only in the resort area, but in nearby Yanchep village and, in particular, in Yanchep National Park. Two Rocks itself has a marine entertainment complex called Atlantis, as well as its share of the superb West Coast beaches. Access to all spots is along a relatively new, sealed highway and even in summer there are no crowds—one of the

The harbour built for an America's Cup challenger now houses a sizeable fishing fleet

delights of the West Australian beach scene that will astound Easterners.

Accommodation is surprisingly limited. There is only the hotel at Two Rocks, not even a camping ground for those who prefer to rough it. The Capricorn Club has an excellent caravan park and camping ground, but that is some seven kilometres down the road towards Yanchep itself. I have always been surprised at the lack of accommodation in the near-city holiday resorts in Western Australia. Similar areas in other parts of Australia are often oversupplied to the point of being aggravating, with caravan parks and motels on virtually every corner.

Despite the lack of accommodation, Two Rocks has as much to offer the vacationing family, as it has the day visitor. It is well worth a trip just to see the 'cradle' of Australia's international yachting success. It is also well worth staying over and enjoying the beaches, the fishing, the bushwalking or whatever else takes your fancy.

By road 60km N of Perth
RAC Depot See Yanchep
Caravan access Sealed road all the way
Best weather October thru' March
Accommodation Club Capricorn Caravan Park
Beaches Superb Coastal beaches
Rock fishing Good
Beach fishing Excellent
Offshore fishing Excellent
Still water fishing Good in harbour
Sailing Good
Sailboarding Excellent
Trailer-sailers Good, easy launching in harbour
Water skiing Limited, open sea only
Canoeing Good, open sea only
Skindiving Excellent on offshore reefs
Fuel and Bait Local store
Boat Hire None
Ramps Excellent ramp in harbour
National Parks Yanchep N P
Interests Original base for America's Cup challengers. Atlantis Dolphin pool. Club Capricorn

YANCHEP

The name Yanchep is synonymous with magnate Alan Bond and his early attempts to win the America's Cup with his yacht *Southern Cross*. However, the real Yanchep is as far removed from such events as honey is from lemon juice. Not in terms of distance, for in fact the town of Yanchep is less than 10 kilometres from the scene of those early brave challenges. But removed in an aesthetic as well as a practical sense, for not only does Yanchep not have all the glitter and glamour that goes with world sporting events, it does not even have a boat ramp.

Yanchep itself is a neat, moderately sized settlement some 50 kilometres north of Perth. Set among the scrub-covered coastal sand dunes, it is a quiet, peaceful spot. So quiet and peaceful one might be forgiven for thinking it had gone to sleep, but far from it, Yanchep is a very up-to-date holiday resort.

Certainly there is no motel, but there is one of the finest caravan and camping resorts on the coast. Set superbly among the coastal

undulations, this resort has virtually its own beach, its own tennis court, horse riding, hang gliding and many other holiday attractions.

Fishermen are well catered for with good beach fishing and excellent offshore reefs that produce spectacular catches. Boats can only be launched at Two Rocks, but the facility there is second to none.

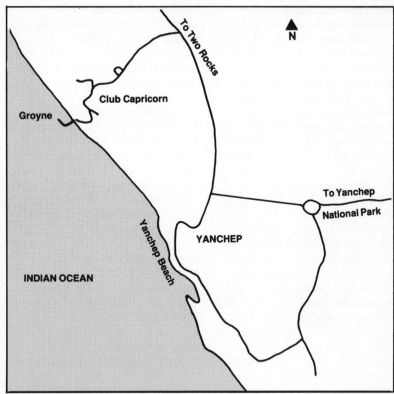

The delightful lagoon at Yanchep

Yanchep National Park caters for bushwalkers and campers while Club Capricorn offers trail riding and hang gliding.

Accommodation is surprisingly limited, but perhaps the fact that none of the attractions is much more than 50 kilometres from the centre of Perth means that they are used more by weekend visitors than those who come to stay. Whatever the reason, I find it hard to believe that many families would not delight in spending a few weeks in an area with so much to offer.

Yanchep National Park has many features beside the natural bush and the swampy lakes, one of which rejoices in the name 'Loch McNess'! There is a good golf course, three ovals, a swimming pool and a boat hire establishment. There is also a hotel/motel, a guest house and a

museum, all quite unique in such a location, buried deep in the heart of a national park.

By road 51km N of Perth
RAC Depot Two Rocks Service Centre, Phone 61 1192, 61 1128
Caravan access Sealed road all the way
Best weather October thru' March
Accommodation 1 hotel/motel, 1 guest house, 1 caravan park
Beaches Yanchep Beach. Coastal beaches
Rock fishing Excellent
Beach fishing Excellent
Offshore fishing See Two Rocks
Still water fishing None
Sailing Excellent, open sea only
Sailboarding Excellent
Trailer-sailers See Two Rocks
Water skiing See Two Rocks
Canoeing Excellent, open sea only
Skindiving Excellent
Fuel and Bait See Two Rocks
Boat hire None
Ramps See Two Rocks
National Parks Yanchep N P
Interests Hang gliding. Golf. Horse riding. Numerous interests in Yanchep National Park

QUINNS

While in some ways similar to neighbouring Burns Beach, Quinns Rocks differs considerably. It does not have the country atmosphere of the beach to the south, nor does it have quite the same attractive scenery. That may sound somewhat exaggerated, for the coastline of Western Australia to the north of Perth changes little over hundreds of kilometres. However, each little settlement has its individual character and there is a most distinctive character about Burns Beach which Quinns Rocks lacks.

Nevertheless, it has something that Burns Beach lacks and that is a launching ramp. Not a very effective one, but nevertheless a launching ramp. Large fishing boats and trailer-sailers could not use it unless they were towed by a four-wheel drive vehicle, for the concrete part of the ramp ends well above the water's edge and at low tide there is a considerable expanse of sand between the ramp and the water. However, it is ideal for small craft such as catamarans and small fishing boats which can be manhandled over the sand, and it provides good access to the water with a large car and trailer parking area nearby.

The early navigators along this coastline feared the treacherous reefs offshore and many came to grief in the boiling surf only a kilometre or so from the shore. Apart from producing superb

Quinns is a typical West Coast beach

catches of fish, these reefs are also proving a treasure-house of old maritime relics, and rarely does a summer go by without a new wreck revealing its long-hidden secrets to divers.

Obviously, skindiving is a prime sport in this region and although the offshore reefs which give Quinns Rocks its name probably have no hidden treasure, they certainly have plenty of fish. Fishermen who launch a boat here are well-rewarded for their efforts. Snapper abound on the reefs, as do a wide variety of palatable fish.

For families on holiday at Quinns Rocks there is just the beach. But what a superb beach it is. Fine silver sand stretching away to the north and south, fronted by a modest breaking sea and backed by scrub-covered sand dunes. Like most beaches along the north coast, Quinns Rocks has only a moderate break, not really enough to be called a surf, yet enough to make for a great deal of fun, especially for the youngsters.

As an alternative to the beach, nearby Neerabup National Park provides a pleasant spot to visit, bushwalk or camp. It is inland from the coast, near the highway, and has easy access. Contact the ranger at Yanchep National Park for further information.

Apart from the caravan park there is no accommodation at Quinns Rocks and the store is the only source of supplies. It is a fairly

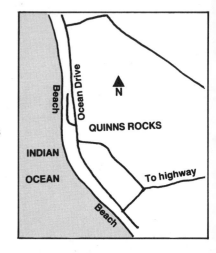

By road	40km N of Perth
RAC Depot	See Yanchep
Caravan access	Sealed road all the way
Best weather	October thru' March
Accommodation	1 caravan park
Beaches	Quinns Beach
Rock fishing	Excellent
Beach fishing	Excellent
Offshore fishing	Excellent, but launching may be difficult
Still water fishing	None
Sailing	Excellent, open sea only
Sailboarding	Excellent
Trailer-sailers	Good, but launching may be difficult
Water skiing	Good, but launching may be difficult
Canoeing	Excellent, open sea only
Skindiving	Excellent
Fuel and Bait	Local store
Boat hire	None
Ramps	Over-beach only
National Parks	Neerabup Lake N P
Interests	Coastal scenery

modern settlement and pleasantly located along the beach. Since Perth is only 40 kilometres away, many visitors come only for the day or weekend, which probably accounts for the limited accommodation on offer.

It is a pleasant place for family beach holidays, but has little to offer beyond sand, sun and surf. Of course that is all many people look for in a holiday spot, so if you fit into that category, then take a trip to Quinns Rocks on your next vacation.

BURNS BEACH

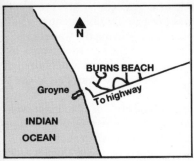

An ideal spot for family holidays within a few kilometres of the city

Although only a few kilometres beyond Perth's outer suburbs, Burns Beach has the atmosphere of being hundreds of kilometres from anywhere. It is a typical small country settlement perched on the coastline seemingly isolated from civilisation by the long stretches of unspoilt beaches and sand dunes that sweep away on either side.

Burns Beach is a little different to most holiday spots on this part of the coast in that it has only a small beach tucked between low cliffs and rocks in the immediate vicinity of the village. On a coastline that seems to consist solely of sand beaches and sand dunes, cliffs and rocky outcrops are rare. However, immediately to the north of Burns Beach, the sand dunes and long beaches pick up again and sweep away to the north virtually out of sight.

The off lying reefs break the worst of the Indian Ocean swell here as they do along the entire north coast of Western Australia. The strong sea breezes do not allow the broken water to rest, however, and mostly a heavy short chop breaks on the beaches. This is a frustrating sea for sports lovers, for it creates sufficient break to be of nuisance value when launching a boat or casting a line, but insufficient to provide good surfing or wave-jumping.

There is no launching ramp at Burns Beach, you will need to go north to Yanchep or south to Ocean Beach for a good ramp. Trailer-sailers can launch at either of these but

the coast in this region has little to offer offshore sailors except danger. The offlying reefs are a very great danger and create a permanent problem for all boatowners in offshore waters.

But what makes for dangerous navigation often provides excellent fishing and the reefs off this coast are no exception. The catches taken from these waters are legendary, but boats that fish offshore must be very seaworthy and their owners very experienced or what could be a rewarding outing may turn into a maritime tragedy.

Fishing from the rocks and beach at Burns Beach can also be a problem for the water is somewhat shallow and, as mentioned, whips up into a nasty chop. However, the fish are there to be had and if you get out early before the sea breeze springs up your chances of taking some decent fish will be much improved.

The beach-loving family will enjoy this pleasant spot most of all. Once away from the rocks, there is ample beach stretching away north as far as the eye can see. Because the surf is not too severe, even youngsters can enjoy the sea without any risk of danger. Children love the chop that gets up in the afternoons, it is just big enough to give them thrills and spills without

any great risk of injury. It will be too much for toddlers, of course, but since there is little undertow they can paddle at the edge.

Outside the beach there is very little at Burns Beach. The caravan park is small and crowded but is the only form of accommodation. Because the coastline is composed almost entirely of sand dunes, even taking a walk literally means a walk along the beach. There is a single small store that caters for day-to-day needs, but nothing else. If you intend to camp you will need to be self-contained.

By road	30km N of Perth
RAC Depot	See Yanchep
Caravan access	Sealed road all the way
Best weather	October thru' March
Accommodation	1 caravan park
Beaches	Burns Beach. Coastal beaches
Rock fishing	Excellent
Beach fishing	Excellent
Offshore fishing	Excellent, but launching may be difficult
Still water fishing	None
Sailing	Good, open sea only
Sailboarding	Excellent
Trailer-sailers	Good, but launching may be difficult
Water skiing	Good, but launching may be difficult
Canoeing	Good, open sea only
Skindiving	Excellent on offshore reefs
Fuel and Bait	Local store
Boat hire	None
Ramps	Over-beach only
National Parks	Neerabup Lake N P
Interests	Coastal scenery

ROTTNEST ISLAND

Most major holiday resorts have been endowed with flattering descriptive names aimed at attracting would-be visitors. Not so Rottnest Island, for who could be attracted to a place with the repulsive name of 'Rat's Nest'! Yet that is the literal translation of the Dutch name given to the Island in 1696 by the explorer Willem de Vlamingh. Of course, de Vlamingh was not to know that the Island would one day become one of Western Australia's prime holiday resorts or he may have given it a more appropriate name. He did, however, appreciate the beauty of the spot, for he noted in his journal:

'Here it seems nature has spared nothing to render this isle delightful above all other islands I did ever see…a terrestial paradise.'

The source of his unusual name was the quokka, a species of short-tailed scrub wallaby unique to Rottnest Island as they are now extinct on the mainland except for a small colony at Bald Head, near Albany. de Vlamingh thought they were large rats and named the Island accordingly. The quokkas not only

survive on the Island, but flourish as they have become a major tourist attraction, mixing freely with human visitors in the region of Thomson Bay.

But the beauty of this delightful island only 18 kilometres across the calm waters of Gage Roadstead from Fremantle was not its attraction in the days of early settlement. It provided the perfect location for a prison and in 1839 the original settlers, Robert Thomson and his family, were returned to the mainland and an Aboriginal penal settlement was established. The prisoners were used to build a small township of limestone buildings, many of which exist to this day and are another attraction for tourists. Recovering salt from the salt lakes that cover much of the eastern half of the Island provided an industry for the prisoners, and this, together with farming, helped the Island become a self-sufficient community.

The developments of those less attractive years in the history of Rottnest Island help to provide much of the interest which makes the Island today far more than a

self-sufficient community, it is a very prosperous tourist centre. The old buildings along the waterfront date back to the late 1830s, most of them residential premises for the Governor and his staff. Part of the prison, known as the Quad, was built in 1864 and for over 10 years housed Aboriginal prisoners who reputedly used the courtyard for their tribal dances and songs. The Quad is now used by tourists who laze and chat in the courtyard and sleep in the cells where once the native prisoners endured squalor and privation.

Other relics of those grim days are to be found all around the island. Far less dramatic than the prison relics but just as unique are the pheasants and peacocks which were originally introduced to the Island to provide sport for the Governor and his guests. Conditions on the Island have suited the birds. Like the quokkas, they have flourished and may be seen at a number of spots away from the settlement area. Rottnest has been a declared animal sanctuary since the days of penal settlement ended and as a result, a wide variety of species,

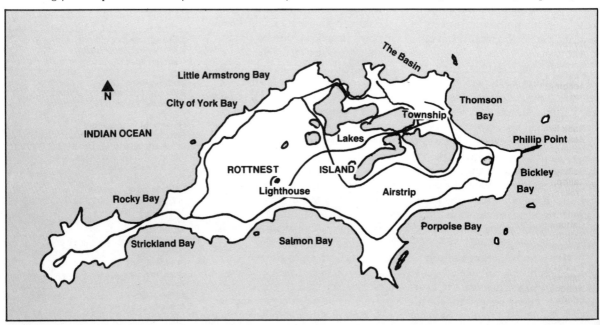

One of the nicest things to do on Rottnest Island is just sit on the beach and meditate!

By road N/A
RAC Depot N/A
Caravan access N/A
Best weather October thru' March
Accommodation 2 hotels, 1 camping ground
Beaches Numerous bays and beaches around Island
Rock fishing Excellent
Beach fishing Excellent
Offshore fishing Excellent
Still water fishing Limited
Sailing Excellent
Sailboarding Excellent
Trailer-sailers Excellent, access via Fremantle
Water skiing Excellent
Canoeing Excellent
Skindiving Excellent
Fuel and Bait Local stores
Boat hire See information bureau at Thomson Bay
Ramps N/A
National Parks None
Interests Historic buildings. Quokkas. Magnificent coastal scenery

particularly sea birds, can be found in the bays and inlets that pockmark the shores. The salt lakes also attract many varieties of birds and small animals. Needless to say, naturalists and wildlife photographers find the Island a paradise.

The salt lakes have another facet of interest to visitors, and that is their high salinity. The water in the lakes is seven times saltier than the sea and therefore has a good buoyancy factor. Some of the smaller lakes are not salt, but contain totally fresh water, and it is interesting to see the contrasting species of wildlife that is attracted to the closely adjacent waterways. Apart from the quokkas, ducks, oyster catchers, herons and a wide variety of birds frequent the fresh water pools.

Since it creates a breakwater for the mainland, Rottnest Island bears the full brunt of the Indian Ocean, for there is no land between this Island and Madagascar, off the continent of South Africa. Much of the fury of the wild Southern Ocean is also blown north to break on the Island's shores. As might be expected from an offshore island in such an exposed position, its geography is rugged. But it is also varied, for the exposed southern side of the Island bears the impact of the ocean's surge while the northern shores are mostly sheltered. Thus on the one side is a typical ocean coast with rugged headlands and deeply indented surf beaches, while on the other the bays and inlets are shallow and sandy with crystal clear water. There could be no more perfect combination for a holiday spot!

While the historic and geographic aspects of Rottnest Island will appeal to most tourists, they are of little interest to small people, to whom a holiday simply means beaches, still water and sun. On this remarkable Island even tiny tots are catered for. There are numerous sheltered bays, particularly across the north side, with lovely sandy beaches and clear still water ideally suited for family holidays. Probably the only problem that might arise in planning a Rottnest Island holiday for the family is finding a place to stay. With around 250,000 visitors a year, most obviously during the holiday season, the Island's accommodation is stretched to the limit. Check your bookings well beforehand if you plan to stay on the Island, or you may be disappointed. Day trips are no problem, of course, since ferries and aircraft run regular schedules from the mainland.

Fishing, sailboarding, sailing, skindiving (but no spearfishing in many places), cruising or just lazing in the sun. It is all there for the individual, for couples and for families. It would be hard to find a more suitable place for a holiday than Rottnest Island and the only factor which might weigh against it is the very factor which ensures its survival—the crowds which visit every year. Only a short distance from the State's capital city and with such easy access, Rottnest has a rosy future ahead of it. A future which, hopefully, will not be marred by excessive development on what is at present one of Australia's most lovely natural islands.

Rottnest Island is an ideal sailaway spot for family yachts such as this Star 700, a popular WA product

PERTH BEACHES

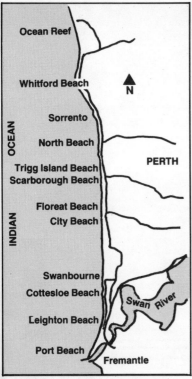

Magnificent beaches stretch along the entire seafront of the city of Perth

Someone once said that the west coast of Australia is just one big beach. This is not strictly true, of course, but neither is it as much of an exaggeration as it may seem. Certainly no other part of the Australian continent has such long, unbroken stretches of beach covering such a vast tract of coastline. And it is not just the length of the beaches, but the remarkably placid nature of the seas that wash them. Certainly there are stretches where surf breaks quite heavily, but for the most part the clean, sandy coastline is fringed by quiet water that breaks heavily only in storm conditions.

This is all the more remarkable since the west coast faces directly towards the stretch of Indian Ocean that reaches unbroken to the coasts of Africa. It is also remarkable since the coastline in many regions is constantly subjected to strong onshore winds, as witness the trees which in many parts of the coast are permanently bent over. An open ocean with a constant wind of some strength is a certain recipe for a rugged, surf-battered coastline and the Bay of Biscay, west coast of Ireland and the Great Australian Bight are living testimony to this. But the west coast of Australia has one feature which those other coastlines lack—an offshore barrier reef. It is this which breaks the fury of the ocean swells some distance out from the coast and creates the moderate surf which breaks on the beaches.

Nowhere is there a more representative stretch of the coastline than that fronting the city of Perth. From Fremantle Harbour to the limit of the city suburbs, some 30 kilometres to the north, there are no less than 15 beaches in a continuous, virtually unbroken stretch. Some have a moderate surf where the reef barrier is broken, some have no more than a ripple playing on their shores.

All have wide, clean, sandy

By road 5—35km from Perth
RAC Depot Phone 325 5566
Caravan access Sealed roads to all points
Best weather October thru' March
Accommodation Full range of city accommodation
Beaches 10 major coastal beaches
Rock fishing Good from outcrops and reefs
Beach fishing Excellent
Offshore fishing Excellent, access via Ocean Reef or Fremantle
Still water fishing Excellent in Swan River
Sailing Excellent in open sea or river
Sailboarding Excellent
Trailer-sailers Excellent, good launching facilities
Water skiing Excellent
Canoeing Excellent in open sea or river
Skindiving Excellent on offshore reefs
Fuel and Bait City and suburban stores
Boat hire See city guide
Ramps Ocean Reef boat harbour. Swan River
National Parks None
Interests Full range of city features

A surf carnival takes place within a few kilometres of the city centre

foreshores backed by sand dunes and fronted with crystal clear turqoise-coloured water. Small craft can put off from most of these beaches and sail or motor directly out to the relatively shallow offshore waters. Most areas produce good catches of fish and all provide excellent diving. If there is any complaint about these beaches, it is likely to come from board riders bemoaning the lack of good-sized surf waves!

There is more of the same to the north and the south, and if one were required to make a criticism, it could only be that there is so much of the same. If it is possible to have a surfeit of a beautiful coastline with

magnificent beaches, then perhaps you could have a surfeit on the west coast of Western Australia!

Astonishingly, some of the finest beaches in this State are to be found along the coastal strip that fronts the city of Perth. They begin right at the port of Fremantle under the shadow of container berths and oil installations. From the port entrance, the first run of silver beach heads northwards beside the railway line. This is Port Beach, a popular spot with Fremantle residents since it fringes the still, clear waters of Gage Roads as it sweeps towards the next stretch of sand, known as Leighton Beach.

Where Leighton Beach sweeps up to Mudurup Rocks, another groyne creates the southern curve of Cottesloe Beach. Here the surf starts to become a little more prominent, although still nothing like the surf experienced on the other side of the continent. North Cottesloe Beach and then Swanbourne Beach are all patrolled and have their surf life-saving clubs. Sailboarding is very popular along this area and late in the afternoon when the sea breeze is up, the water is covered with a speckled rash of colourful sails.

At this point, the road cuts inland and the suburban sprawl comes to an end. The beach continues northwards without a break and without changing its pattern of wide, white sand backed by high dunes. But behind the beach is bushland, giving the effect of a coastal strip from the country areas, far removed from a major city. In fact, this strip of virtually unspoiled coast is less than 10 kilometres from the very centre of the city! It has one unique feature I have not seen on any other city beach in the form of a strip of beach for exercising animals. Not just dogs and other normally banned animals, but horses and whatever other animal you may wish to exercise. Only in a city with such a wealth of beaches could such a thing be possible. Nudists are apparently not considered in the animal category since they are not permitted anywhere!

Northwards the beaches march on unhindered and virtually unchanged. Civilisation comes back at City Beach although the

The excellent boat harbour at Ocean Reef

suburban clutter is kept a little farther back than before, allowing a wide swathe of dunes between the beach and the houses. Floreat Beach is long and delightful, then comes the famous Scarborough Beach with its massive resort buildings towering above the beach. Trigg Island Beach has a little headland and rocks to break the monotonous progression of beach and dunes, but the sand continues on the northern side with now a modest surf, but still the brilliant white sand and clear, turqoise water. North Beach, Waterman's Beach, Marmion Beach and Sorrento Beach make up the next sweep of sand-fringed coastline until the new Hillarys Boat Harbour brings it to a sudden stop.

But only briefly, for the beaches on this coastline are interminable. To the north of Sorrento is Whitford Beach, Mullaloo Beach, with its popular water-skiing area, and Ocean Reef, where again the progression of sand and dunes is broken

by a boat harbour. This is an excellent harbour with first-class facilities for all sizes of boats, including trailer-sailers, and provides an immediate access to the offshore waters. It is widely used by fishermen heading out to the prolific offshore reefs, and on summer weekends the ramps and basin can become quite congested. The new boat harbour at Sorrento, which had still to be completed at the time of my survey, may relieve some of this congestion.

At Ocean Reef the suburbs of Perth finally give up and as the beaches continue their march northwards they are now backed by more natural, more aesthetic countryside. There is access to these beaches only by four-wheel drive vehicles, and then only at certain points. Conventional vehicles must head inland and pick up the northbound highway which will carry them to the individual turn-offs of the small beach resorts along the coast to the north of Perth.

FREMANTLE

When Fremantle was first determined as the Australian venue for the 1987 defence of the coveted America's Cup, potential challengers from yacht clubs all over the world thumbed through their atlases to locate the unheard-of town and found it in very small writing close to Perth. Even Australians—particularly 'Easterners'—tended to think of Fremantle as 'somewhere near Perth', for when the days of big passenger liners and crowded emigrant ships ended, the once-busy port on the west coast fell into a dormant limbo, mentioned only rarely in conversations or newspaper columns.

Australia's success in the America's Cup challenge changed all that. The historic town at the mouth of the Swan River is now a household word, not only nationally, but also internationally. Not since it was first established as a military deterrent against French ambitions in Western Australia has Fremantle been so much the focus of attention. And once again the delightfully innocuous little town has written itself into Australian history books, albeit this time through its sporting rather than its military connections.

It was master navigator Matthew Flinders who was indirectly responsible for the establishment of a settlement on the west coast of Australia. In 1801 he circumnavigated the continent proving that the west coast was part of the land already settled and claimed as a British colony. In the course of his expedition, Flinders encountered the French expedition of Nicolas Baudin and reported that the French navigator has extensively explored the west coast. Fearful that their erstwhile enemies might lay claim to this side of the continent, the British established a settlement at Albany in 1826 and in 1829 a colony was formed at the

mouth of the Swan River and named after the naval captain who formally took possession in the name of the Crown.

As the westernmost port on the Australian continent, Fremantle thrived from its conception. Even when the nearby upstart town of Perth grew rapidly to become the capital of Western Australia, Fre-

mantle retained its importance as the port of entry for most trade entering Australia. It reached its zenith in the days when travel between Europe and Australia was almost purely by sea, berthing some of the world's finest liners at its riverside wharves. Shipping schedules to the southern continent invariably listed Fremantle as the

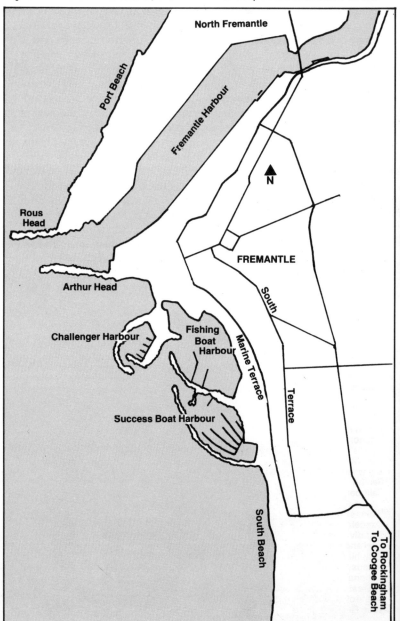

The history of Fremantle is preserved in its fine buildings

By road   18km SW of Perth
RAC Depot   Cnr South Tce and Price St, Phone 325 5566
Caravan access   Sealed road to all points
Best weather   October thru' March
Accommodation   Wide range of city accommodation available
Beaches   Fremantle Beach. Cockburn Beach. Coogee Beach
Rock fishing   Good from breakwaters and outcrops
Beach fishing   Excellent
Offshore fishing   Excellent, good access
Still water fishing   Good from jetties and wharves
Sailing   Excellent
Sailboarding   Excellent
Trailer-sailers   Excellent
Water skiing   Excellent
Canoeing   Excellent
Skindiving   Excellent
Fuel and Bait   Town or local stores
Boat hire   None
Ramps   Fremantle. Cockburn
National Parks   None
Interests   Historic buildings in town. Scene of America's Cup defence in harbour. Fishing fleet

first port of call on the outward bound journey, and last port of call on the return passage. It was truly the gateway to Australia.

After 150 years of prominence, however, the Western Australian port began to slip into limbo as booming air travel spelled an end to the stately liners. Cargo-carrying freighters still berthed in the Swan River mouth, but these, too, were decreasing in numbers each year. The small fishing boat fleet struggled to maintain a busy trade, but as with all major shipping ports around the world, the writing was on the wall for Fremantle, and its trade declined dramatically.

However, in the bustling years since the first settlement, the town had quietly developed its character. Many of its early buildings were retained and the charm of the old town was not affected by the growth of new buildings. Nowadays Fremantle is a delightful historic centre attracting tourists with its nostalgia and charm and gradually building up a new and viable industry in tourism. Unfortunately both Perth and Fremantle are off the beaten track as far as world tourism is concerned. Aircraft do not enter Australia from the west, as did the old ships. Some catalyst was needed to literally 'put Fremantle on the map', and elucidate its charms to the world at large and tourists in particular.

That catalyst was the triumph of Western Australia's Alan Bond in winning the world's top yachting trophy, the America's Cup, in 1983. Bond and the Royal Perth Yacht Club named Gage Roads, off the port of Fremantle, as the venue for the 1987 defence of the Cup, and Fremantle as the base for the event. Suddenly the historic little town was hurtled back into the public spotlight. Few events, sporting or otherwise, could have been better planned to revive Fremantle's waning fortunes. Overnight it became virtually the tourist centre of Australia with its waterfront once again being the focal point.

Apart from the vastly (and quickly) changed scene along the foreshores and in the boat harbours, Fremantle has much to offer the visitor. Its historic old buildings have an individual charm while the town as a whole is little changed from the days when tall funnels and masts towered above the wharf sheds and steam trains chuffed out of the delightful Victorian station in a cloud of soot and smoke. The masts, the funnels and the steam trains are gone, now, but Fremantle retains an atmosphere in its narrow streets and rows of old houses which almost seems to recreate those nostalgic days. History enthusiasts will have a field day in this town, starting with the Round House, which was originally built in 1831 as a gaol, and encompassing such delights as the elegant Town Hall (1887), the Fremantle Markets and the adjacent Warders' Quarters in Henderson Street.

Families who find their holiday interest more aligned to sun, water and the big outdoors will equally find it hard to know where to start. The Fishing Boat Harbour is the scene of the America's Cup activities and caters for all tastes, ranging from those who just like to nosey about and see what is going on, to those who prefer to watch from the luxury of a sophisticated waterfront restaurant. Adjacent boat harbours to the north and south provide even more maritime interest with access to the water for those who bring their own boats. South Fremantle Beach is small but ideal for families, since it has clean sand and clear water with next to no surf, even when the wind is up.

Across the bay is Garden Island, the original spot where the first settlers landed, but now a naval base and inaccessible by road without permission. Between the Island and the mainland lies a still stretch of water named Cockburn Sound and it is here that numerous water activities take place. Just south of Fremantle, the beaches sweep around the edge of the Sound in a

long ribbon of fine sand. Coogee Beach is popular, while to the south again, access to sea is provided via a superb launching ramp and boat harbour at Woodman Point. There is also a delightful beach here for those who do not wish to take to the water.

Much of Fremantle is a strange mix of industry and recreation, and the beaches to the south are no exception. The sandy ribbon continues around the curve of Cockburn Sound but it is broken by boat building yards, chemical factories and oil refineries. The town is a similar mix, with the shipping wharves located close to interesting craft shops that fringe the main shopping centre. The forbidding grey walls of the gaol frown down on everything, adding a sombre note to the gay colours of the shops and markets and the pleasant greenery of the trees in the town centre. There is much to see and do just in the town of Fremantle. The combination of town and waterfront attractions must rate as top tourist value, not only in the western State, but anywhere in Australia.

An International 12 metre class yacht prepares for the America's Cup challenge races in Fremantle Boat Harbour

ROCKINGHAM

Few Western Australian towns have had a more colourful and varied past than Rockingham. In the first instance the town was located in the wrong place and had to be moved. Then the timber cutters in the hills of the hinterland decided to make it the port for the Jarrah cargoes, so it was in effect moved back again. For many years it was a major export outlet for the timber and the old jetty often berthed two or three big windjammers at the one time.

But as time went by, ports further south took over the role of shipping the timber and Rockingham fell back into limbo again. The causeway linking Garden Island naval base with the mainland brought some trade, but it was tourism which once again brought the fine old timber port back into prominence. And with tourism booming by the year, Rockingham, like many of the ghost ports along the West Coast, seems destined to

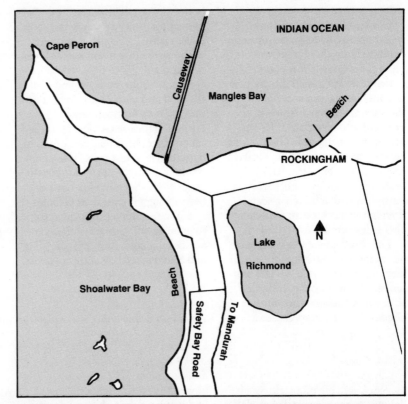

By road 46km S of Perth
RAC Depot Rockingham Park Mobil Service, Phone 27 2092, 27 6009
Caravan access Sealed highway
Best weather November thru' February
Accommodation 1 hotel/motel, 1 hotel, 1 private hotel, 5 caravan parks
Beaches Rockingham beach. Shoalwater Bay. Safety Bay
Rock fishing Excellent
Beach fishing Excellent
Offshore fishing Excellent
Still water fishing Good from jetty
Sailing Excellent
Sailboarding Excellent
Trailer-sailers Good. Launching may be difficult for large craft
Water skiing Excellent
Canoeing Excellent
Skindiving Excellent
Fuel and Bait Town stores
Boat hire On waterfront
Ramps Good ramps on Esplanade and on W side of causeway
National Parks None
Interests Historic buildings in township. Cape Peron. Causeway to Garden Island

A peaceful corner of Shoalwater Bay

enjoy a prosperous future.

Close to Perth and with every requirement for a casual visit or an extended stay, Rockingham is a natural for tourists throughout the entire year. For casual day trippers the brilliant turquoise of Shoalwater Bay provides a beach scene not unlike that of the Barrier Reef. The similarity is heightened by the wide beach of fine sand and the dotted islands that shelter the Bay. Catch Shoalwater Bay on a brilliant, sunny day and you have a scene from a travel poster with colours almost beyond belief.

The town side of Cape Peron is not quite so beautiful, but it is still ideal for family holidays. The sea, broken down almost to millpond stillness by the giant breakwater of Garden Island and its causeway, is perfect for small children. It is also perfect for almost every water sport except surfing. So still is the surface of the water that even water-skiers revel on it.

It is also quite shallow, and while this is ideal for small children, it can be annoying for boatowners. Although the area is ideal for trailer-sailers, launching may be a problem, particularly at low tide. The ramps on the Esplanade are good, but the water at the bottom may not be deep enough if your boat is large.

Sailing, sailboarding, canoeing, swimming; all are part of the scene at Rockingham. Both Mangles Bay and Shoalwater Bay come alive on sunny weekends with colourful sails dotting the brilliant aqua-coloured water. At low tide you can walk out to Penguin Island across the shallows, but if you do so be careful of the bar, for it can be dangerous.

Rockingham is an interesting town with many historic buildings so there are plenty of activities other than those connected with the beach or the water. But it is the lovely sand and water which appeals most to holidaymakers and which provide such fun for the kids. It is a wonderful spot for a quick visit or a week's holiday, for it has something to suit everybody and that is what holidays are all about.

The beaches to the north of Rockingham are cluttered with heavy industry

SOUTHERN BEACHES

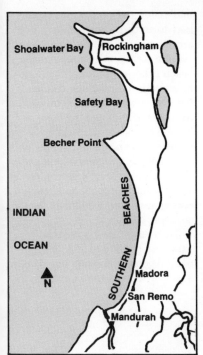

One might say that the whole of the Western Australian coast is one big beach, and nowhere is this better illustrated than on the stretch of coast that runs south from Mandurah to Bunbury. Having withstood the batterings of the Indian Ocean for centuries, the coast has built up a heavy line of defences in the form of sand dunes, some of them 50-70 metres high. What is unique about these sand dunes is that they run inland for some distance, often a few kilometres from the line of the ocean.

Behind the sand dunes, as is so often the case, a series of shallow lakes has developed, creating a haven for wildfowl of many species. The largest of these lakes is Peel Inlet which breaks through to the coast at Mandurah, but this is an extensive, major waterway whereas most of the others are relatively small lakes.

The sum total of this unusual handiwork of nature is a magnificent natural coastal wonderland that is the delight of every visitor, particularly those who enjoy unspoiled natural areas. For although there is access to the coast

A typical beach scene south of Rockingham

in a few places, and even a few small settlements among the dunes, this area has been mostly carefully protected so that it will not be damaged by uncaring visitors.

The beach and frontal dunes

By road   Approx 66km S of Perth
RAC Depot   See Mandurah
Caravan access   Sealed road to all points
Best weather   November thru' February
Accommodation   1 caravan park (San Remo)
Beaches   Superb coastal beaches
Rock fishing   Limited
Beach fishing   Excellent
Offshore fishing   Excellent, but launching may be difficult
Still water fishing   Limited in Serpentine River
Sailing   Excellent
Sailboarding   Excellent
Trailer-sailers   Launching too difficult
Water skiing   Good, but launching may be difficult
Canoeing   Good, open sea or Serpentine River
Skindiving   Excellent on offshore reefs
Fuel and Bait   Local stores
Boat hire   None
Ramps   Over-beach only in a few spots
National Parks   Serpentine N P
Interests   Superb coastal beach scenery

must be much as they were when the first white explorers sailed along the coast. Standing on the firm but fine white sand, you can look north and south and see nothing but unbroken beach and dunes disappearing into the haze of distance. What is more, you will probably not see a solitary person along that unbroken line of beach. The few people who do visit are swallowed up in the vastness of the distance.

It follows, then, that a visit to this spectacular coast is one you should not miss. There is virtually no accommodation (1 small caravan park) along some 80 kilometres of this beach, so although a day trip from Perth is easy, to really enjoy the many delights of this area, it would be better to stay in Mandurah and make a series of forays to different spots.

As a holiday spot it is limited by the lack of accommodation, but a run down the highway from Mandurah takes only half and hour or so, and a day at one of these beaches will make a popular addition to a family holiday at Mandurah. The beaches—they are really just one long beach but are named in sections—are beautiful, the dunes magnificent and the water crystal clear. There is a moderate surf as a rule, but not enough to create danger except for the very young.

Swimming is the main interest since there is little access for boats.

Sailboards and canoes may be carried down through the dunes, but any larger craft will have problems. Fishing is easy, of course, and the beach is known to reward patient fishermen, for some fine catches have been taken here. In the dunes, the lakes behind and the bush behind the lakes, the wildlife is undisturbed and prolific. Particularly in evidence are the wildfowl, for the shallow, reedy lakes provide a good source of food, and pelicans, cormorants, swans and wild ducks are always around.

The coastal area along this stretch of the West Coast is a natural gem. Make sure you do not miss it when visiting Mandurah.

Sailboarding is easy from all these beaches

MANDURAH

Mandurah is derived from the Aboriginal name 'Mandjar', meaning 'trading post'. The early settlers bartered with the natives, using ornaments and tools in exchange for labour. One of Western Australia's earliest pioneers adopted the Aboriginal name when he settled on land in the area. Thomas Peel was thought to have been lost at sea when he did not show up to claim land he had selected near the colony at Fremantle. When he finally did arrive, he was given 101,121 hectares (250,000 acres) between the coast and the Darling Range instead of his original grant.

That land now encompasses the prime holiday town of Mandurah and its extensive waterway known as Peel Inlet. There are few more divergent waterways on the West Coast, for it is possible to enjoy literally every watersport here. The offshore waters provide excellent skindiving, sailing and water-skiing, while the placid waters of the lake provide a relaxing alternative for the less intrepid. Perhaps the only sport not fully catered for is surfing, since the waters along this strip of the coast are not as rugged as they are farther south.

For the day visitor and the tourist alike, the lake cruises are a must. Apart from providing a pleasant few hours on the water, these cruises reveal the enormous extent of this land-locked waterway. There are dozens of hire-boat centres around the perimeter of the Inlet and in the town area, so if you prefer it, then hire a boat and do your own sightseeing.

As far as swimming is concerned, there is quite a variety on offer. Modest surf may be found along the northern or southern beaches away from the town itself, while close to the Inlet entrance is still water ideally suited for kiddies. Around the perimeter there are a few beaches although somehow 'inland'

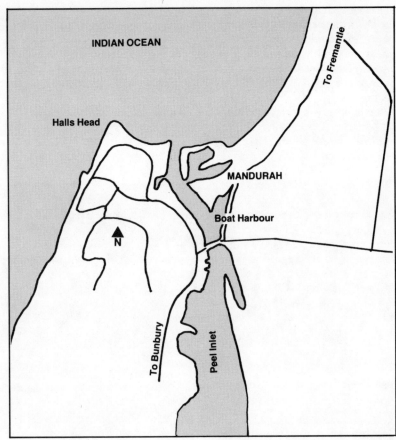

beaches never seem to have quite the same appeal for youngsters as do ocean beaches. But for splashing around just about any old beach will do, and no matter how fussy your child, there will be a beach to suit him or her in Mandurah.

The fishing is just as diversified. If you like braving the open ocean then the reefs off the coast will provide an abundance of fish. Few coastlines in the world are as well provided with offshore reefs as is the west coast, and fishermen take full advantage of them. There is a good launching ramp in the main harbour near the bridge and there are others at strategic points around the Inlet. Access to sea is relatively easy through the breakwater arms although, as usual, care is always necessary when putting out to sea in small boats.

By Road 75km S of Perth
RAC depot In township
Caravan access Sealed highway all the way
Best weather November thru' February
Accommodation 5 hotels, 7 motels, 12 caravan parks
Beaches Coastline is virtually one long beach
Rock fishing Poor
Beach fishing Excellent
Offshore fishing Excellent. Access easy through Peel Estuary
Still water fishing Excellent in Peel Inlet
Sailing Excellent
Sailboarding Excellent
Trailer-Sailers Excellent
Water-skiing Excellent
Canoeing Excellent
Skindiving Excellent in offshore waters
Fuel and bait Town stores
Boat hire Boatsheds on either side of Peel Estuary and Inlet
Ramps Boat Harbour and at points around Inlet foreshores
National parks See Yalgorup
Interests Numerous holiday interests in town and suburbs

Mandurah has one of the most extensive waterways on the south-west coast

For those who prefer the quieter side of fishing, Peel Inlet provides the answer. Or you can fish the beaches or the rocky outcrops at points along the coast. The old saying that wherever there is water there is fish holds good here, and few fishermen return with only the proverbial wet bottom!

There are delightful parks around the foreshores of the waterway, particularly in the town area. There are also amusement parks for the youngsters as well as the usual swings and slippery dips. Accommodation, like everything else in Mandurah, covers the full range, from caravan parks to elegant and expensive resort complexes. Thomas Peel would smile in his grave if he realised what a well-organised town he had spawned.

Mandurah is only an hour's drive from Perth so it is an easy town to take in for a day trip. But there is so much to see and do in the area, that it would seem a pity not to spend longer and enjoy it all. One of Western Australia's finest waterways cannot really be fully enjoyed in a day.

YALGORUP COAST

The long sweep of the southern beaches is broken briefly at Mandurah by the entrance to Peel Inlet. Since Halls Head, the protrusion which protects the entrance from the prevailing south-westerly winds, is surrounded by beaches and the entrance itself is very narrow, there is very little interruption to the remarkable sandy ribbon which runs for almost two hundred kilometres south along the coast from Perth to Busselton. Built up over centuries by the relentless action of the Indian ocean, this remarkable area of sandy beaches and sand dunes has created a buffer between the land mass and the ocean.

Nowhere is the geological structure of this coastal region more in evidence than along the coastal strip south of Mandurah. For almost 100 kilometres the long sweep of

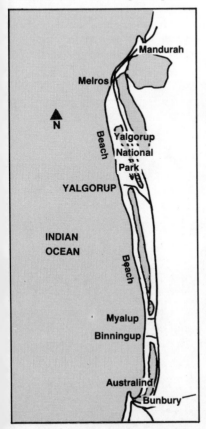

The Leschenault Inlet is one of many waterways that lie behind the sand dunes

coast is comprised of virtually one magnificent sandy beach fronting directly onto the Indian ocean. Backing this beach are high sand dunes, mostly covered with some sort of vegetation and behind these are secondary dunes, the results of eons of conflict between the sea and the land.

Locked behind the dunes is a chain of salt lakes, typical of this type of coastal structure, and found in many places around the continent. These lakes are shallow and reed-fringed, providing the perfect habitat for wildfowl of a number of species as well as coastal wildflowers and fauna. Behind the lakes come the coastal forests which extend inland to the ranges and which in many cases have been cleared by timber-cutters or farmers and replaced by lush pastures. Here man has changed in a few years what nature has taken thousands of years to build.

By road Approx 95km S of Perth
RAC Depot See Mandurah or Bunbury
Caravan access Approx 10km good gravel road from highway to Yalgorup
Best weather November thru' February
Accommodation 2 caravan parks at Australind
Beaches One continuous ocean beach
Rock fishing Very limited
Beach fishing Excellent
Offshore fishing Excellent but access difficult
Still water fishing Limited in lakes and inlets
Sailing Excellent
Sailboarding Excellent
Trailer-sailers Fair in Leschenault Inlet
Water skiing Good at Australind
Canoeing Excellent in lakes or open sea
Skindiving Excellent on offshore reefs
Fuel and Bait Local stores
Boat hire Australind
Ramps Limited over-beach ramps. Inlet ramp at Australind
National Parks Yalgorup N P
Interests Yalgorup National Park interests. Historic buildings at Australind

With careful planning, it is not difficult for man to cohabit with nature, and some careful planning has been applied to this region. To ensure that not all of nature's handiwork is changed, a stretch of this coastline to the south of Mandurah has been declared a national park so that future generations of Australians may observe and study at first hand this remarkable coastal structure. Yalgorup National Park encompasses some of the coastline, the dune and lake systems and some of the hinterland forest. It is a remarkable region, and one which will ensure that whatever development takes place along the coast in future, the sand dune structure will be preserved.

At this stage in time, however, there is little fear of damage to this particular environment. Although the farmers have cleared some of the forests, the sand dune and beach structure is untouched. Only in a few remote spots is there any habitation and with these exceptions, the beach facing the ocean is

little changed from the days before Nicolas Baudin explored this coastline. It is a perfect spot for a get-away-from-it-all holiday with the only problem one of accommodation, for there is not even a caravan park along much of this coast. Perhaps this is the way to keep beaches in their natural state, for only those who make the effort to travel—north from Bunbury or south from Mandurah—will enjoy the solitude of these magnificent beaches or Yalgorup National Park.

Since there is no accommodation, although some camping is permitted in places, it follows that most holiday activities relate to the outdoors. Beach fishing is excellent, as is offshore fishing if you can launch your boat. There is access to the water here and there, but there are no constructed ramps and launching a boat from a trailer must be done over the beach and this requires a four-wheel drive vehicle unless the boat and trailer are very light. Swimming in the clear,

unpolluted water is superb, and there is even a certain amount of surf. Offshore reefs break the ocean swell along the coast in many places, but some good surf waves sneak through occasionally.

The Yalgorup Coast is a perfect spot for families who like their holidays on the beach, away from the madding throng. That also means, of course, away from any facilities, for the lack of caravan parks and crowds means also a lack of stores and other amenities. You will need to take with you what you need for the day unless you visit a spot along the northern stretch where some of the 'suburbs' of Mandurah provide the necessary requirements. It is also a perfect holiday spot for those who like to study nature in its many forms. The wildfowl of the lakes, the lakes themselves, the wildlife and wildflowers of the hinterland and the infra-structure of the dunes all provide superb material for those whose interest lies in this area.

Apart from its beaches, Yalgorup National Park is renowned for its wildflowers

BUNBURY

Many features of the south-west coastline of Western Australia carry French names, the result of the exploration carried out in 1801 by French navigator Nicolas Baudin. He paid particularly close attention to the south-west region where the coast curves westwards and northwards. The bight formed by this curve of land he called Geographe Bay after his own ship, and the tip of the curve he named Cape Naturaliste after the second ship in his expedition. To an inlet he gave the name Port Leschenault, after his naturalist.

It was not until 1836 that settlers began moving into the district, following inspection of the area by Lieutenant William StPierre Bunbury, whose name was later given to

By road 175km S of Perth
RAC Depot Branch Office, Phone 21 2323
Caravan access Sealed road all the way
Best weather November thru' February
Accommodation 7 caravan parks, 7 motels, 5 hotel/motels, 4 hotels, 3 guest houses
Beaches Koombana Beach. Back Beach. Hungry Hollow Beach
Rock fishing Good
Beach fishing Excellent
Offshore fishing Excellent. Easy access through harbour
Still water fishing Good in harbour
Sailing Excellent
Sailboarding Excellent
Trailer-sailers Excellent
Water skiing Excellent
Canoeing Excellent
Skindiving Excellent
Fuel and Bait Town stores
Boat hire See Australind
Ramps Good ramps in harbour
National Parks None
Interests Fine historic buildings. Vintage steam railway. Wildlife parks

the settlement on Leschenault Inlet. Planned as a military outpost, Bunbury was the only possible site for a viable port in the Geographe Bay region, although an earlier settlement had been established at Bussleton. The new port was a natural outlet for the timber hauled out to the coast from the massive forests of the hinterland and the produce of the farmer settlers in the area.

Today Bunbury is still a major seaport and timber is still its major

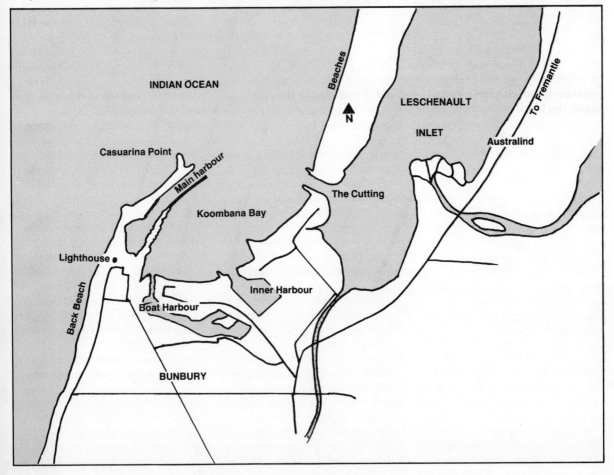

Typical of the fine buildings in Bunbury is the Captain Bunbury Hotel

export, although the timber is now mostly in the form of woodchip. Two-thirds of Western Australia's hardwood forests are located in the region and the woodchip development has brought a new prosperity to the forestry industry which had fallen badly into the doldrums. Other products shipped through the port of Bunbury include mineral sands, mined from the adjacent coastal strips, and products from the rich inland agricultural region.

But over and above its industrial activities, Bunbury is a fast-developing tourist town. Recent years have seen a rapid increase in the number of city vacationers visiting Bunbury for their annual holidays as well as transient visitors touring the delightful south-west coastal region of the State. Bunbury's magnificent

beaches, interesting historic buildings and fine harbour provide attractions for all ages and interests, while its range of accommodation and good shopping facilities give it added appeal as a holiday centre. There are not too many cities where you can stay at a luxury hotel and take only a short walk down to a magnificent sandy beach, nor are there many ports where you can launch almost any size of boat and take your choice of the open sea or a sheltered inlet for your sailing activities.

Add to that the appeal of unlimited beaches running north and south as far as the eye can see, fishing from jetties, the beach and rocky outcrops or in the open sea, and a hinterland with a wide range of natural and industrial activities.

Add also a choice of surf or quiet water for swimming, luxury motels or camping grounds for accommodation. There are so many features about Bunbury that will appeal to holidaying families as well as to tourists, that it is small wonder it is considered one of the major vacation centres on the south-west coast. Together with Mandurah, 100 kilometres to the north, and Busselton, only 50 kilometres to the south, Bunbury forms the nucleus of a superb coastal strip, well-organised for tourists and holidaymakers.

As already mentioned, the beaches in this vacation city are first-class. Ocean Beach and Hungry Hollow Beach front the town on the western side with superb sand, moderate surf and pleasant foreshores. A surf life-saving club is centrally located on these beaches, while the unbroken sandy coastline to the north and south provide unlimited ocean beaches for those who prefer to get away from the crowds. For quiet-water swimming there is Koombana Beach and Harbour Beach, both contained within the arms of the Koombana Bay.

It goes without saying that these waters are ideal for sailing, with a choice of the open sea or sheltered harbour and inlet waters. There is a yacht club and sailing club right in the harbour area, with an excellent launching ramp and full facilities capable of taking even large craft. Access to sea is easy and safe through the main harbour entrance, while the harbour itself provides excellent still water, well-sheltered from the prevailing south-westerly winds by Casuarina Point. Sailing, sailboarding, canoeing and water-skiing are all part of the water scene at Bunbury, with offshore fishing a major boating interest.

Off-water sports activities cover the full range including tennis, bowls, croquet, golf, indoor cricket, etc. Historic old buildings provide another feature of interest away from the water, for Bunbury and its associated countryside is well-endowed with relics of the past. The fine old timber jetty in the harbour is a good starting point, having been first commenced in 1864 and extended from time to time until 1957 when it reached its ultimate length of 1830 metres. The Rose Hotel, built in 1865, and St Marks Church (1841), are but two of numerous buildings that preserve the nostalgia of Bunbury's past. King Cottage Museum (1880) houses a valuable collection of pioneer material.

One could go on at length about the offerings of this southern port city. In a book such as this there is no room to describe all the features that are available to the visitor. Sufficient to say that for a pleasant and interesting holiday, or just for a passing visit, Bunbury has much to offer. Whether you enjoy the sun and the water, or whether your interest lies more with the historical side of the city, you will not be disappointed. There is something in Bunbury for all tastes and there is something for all ages. It is a city that should be prominently located in your holiday diary.

The delightful coastal scenery of Cape Naturaliste is just across the bay from Bunbury

BUSSELTON

When settler John Garrett Bussell landed on the beach in Geographe Bay in 1824 there was no town and no main street. Indeed, there was nothing at all since the Bussells and their party were the first settlers in the district. Not far from the beach is the River Vasse, and John Bussell's first move after landing his party was to cut a track from the beach to the river. That track remains to this day as the main street of the town of Busselton.

The Bussells deserved to have a town named after them, for they were pioneers in the fullest sense of

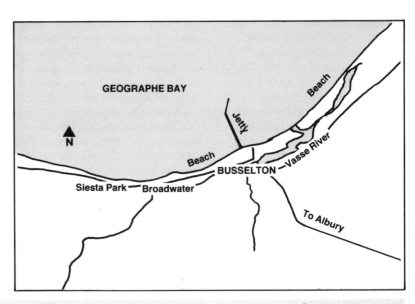

Busselton's historic old jetty once serviced tall windjammers

the word. Son of a clergyman, John Bussell sailed from England in 1829 with a number of his brothers, intent on finding a new and prosperous home for themselves and their families. They landed at Augusta, on the south-west tip of Australia but their early years of settlement were disasterous. Crops failed and they were harrassed by the natives. Their promised land was a complete disappointment.

Lacking nothing in the way of fortitude, the Bussells and their fellow settlers at Augusta determined to try again. This time farther to the north where John Bussell had already applied for a grant of land on the banks of the Vasse River. In 1834 they arrived and cut their now-famous track which was to be the foundation of the town of Busselton. To their astonishment, they discovered a cow that had wandered from their Augusta settlement and somehow found its way almost 100 kilometres north through thick forest and was contentedly grazing on the banks of the Vasse. It seemed that this was an omen, so the Bussells built their homestead on the spot and called it 'Cattle Chosen'!

Busselton quickly developed when the timber cutters moved into the forests of the south-west region. Although located on a fairly shallow, exposed part of the coast, Busselton was chosen as the port from which the timber was shipped. A long jetty was built out from the shore to service the windjammers which either lay in the bay or, if small enough, berthed alongside the jetty head. The jetty stands to this day and is a focal point for tourists, particularly fishermen. For many decades, Busselton thrived as a busy port, providing an outlet for the rapidly developing rural industries of the hinterland as well as for

the timber. But as with most of the small coastal ports, the declining timber industry and the development of road and rail systems saw the fortunes of the port decline to the point where, nowadays, Busselton is just a ghost port.

However, once again like many other small ports along this coastline, tourism took over from commerce and Busselton experienced a new surge of interest with the thousands of holidaymakers that visited the area. The superb scenery of the coastline to the south-west of the town attracts many visitors who use Busselton as a jumping-off spot. The beaches and still waters of Geographe Bay attract many more. Fishing and diving in the offshore waters are excellent, as witness the fact that Busselton supports a sizeable fishing industry, and there is a wide range of beaches on either side of the town. Add to this the historic interest of many of the buildings in the area and the attractive rural hinterland, and you have the reason why Busselton is enjoying a continuing boom in tourism.

For family holidays there is almost everything one could wish for. The beaches, already mentioned, are an example. There is fairly still water in the vicinity of the town and along the southern shores of Geographe Bay towards Dunsborough. Literally dozens of camping settlements have made their base along this shoreline, some of them commercial van parks and camping grounds, other private or charity organisations providing opportunities for pleasant beach holidays for youth and disadvantaged families. The water is so shallow and still on some of these beaches that canoes and other small craft can launch directly into the Bay with

little problems other than the onset of strong winds.

To the north-east of Busselton there are beaches of a totally different calibre. Lacking the sheltering effect of Cape Naturaliste, these beaches face directly to the Indian Ocean and are, for the most part, formed of wide sandy stretches disappearing away into the distance and backed with high sand dunes. A modest surf breaks on these beaches and boat launching facilities are not readily available, being limited almost entirely to an occasional break in the sand dunes where boats can be launched over the sand with a four-wheel drive vehicle. Peppermint Grove Beach and Forrest Beach are two small settlements along this delightful sandy coastline, each providing access to the beach and water, but with only limited facilities, such as a sole caravan park at Peppermint Grove Beach.

By road   228km S of Perth
RAC Depot   Bonded Brakes Busselton, Phone 52 1887, 52 2058
Caravan access   Sealed road all the way
Best weather   November thru' February
Accommodation   7 motels, 1 hotel, 3 hotel/motels, 6 guest houses, 12 caravan parks
Beaches   Town Beach. Peppermint Beach
Rock fishing   Good
Beach fishing   Excellent
Offshore fishing   Excellent
Still water fishing   Excellent from jetty
Sailing   Excellent
Sailboarding   Excellent
Trailer-sailers   Good, but launching may be difficult
Water skiing   Excellent
Canoeing   Excellent
Skindiving   Excellent on offshore reefs
Fuel and Bait   Town stores
Boat hire   None
Ramps   Over-beach ramps or town foreshore
National Parks   None
Interests   Historic old jetty. Old buildings in township

DUNSBOROUGH

Where the broad sweep of Geographe Bay runs round towards Cape Naturaliste, the water gets shallower and the land gets higher. The beach peters out and is replaced by ragged granite headlands, between which are delightful coves. The whole effect gives the huge bluff of Cape Naturaliste a scalloped appearance rather like the rugged Atlantic coasts of France.

This is not the reason why the south-west region of Western Australia has many French names, for the area was first explored by a French expedition under the command of Nicolas Baudin in 1801. While Baudin's name appears rarely, if ever, along the coastline, many of the names relate to his expedition. Cape Geographe is named after his

Still, shallow waters make Dunsborough an ideal spot for children

own ship, while Cape Naturaliste is named after the second ship in his expedition. Freycinet and Hamelin, both common names along the coastline, were both captains under Baudin, while Leschenault was the expedition's botanist.

Some of the earliest white men in the area were only transient settlers. They were the whalers and sealers who decimated the marine life. A whaling operation was established in one of the small coves indented into the western side of Geographe Bay. A large rock they named Castle Rock gave its name to the operation—The Castle Rock Whaling Company. For many years the company operated from this spot, but now nothing remains other than Castle Rock itself and a cairn recording the history of the whalers.

Tucked right into this corner of the Bay, adjacent to Castle Rock Bay, as it is now called, is the village of Dunsborough. It is a neat little holiday centre with a delightful beach, shallow water and good facilities. It makes an excellent spot for family holidays for the shallow,

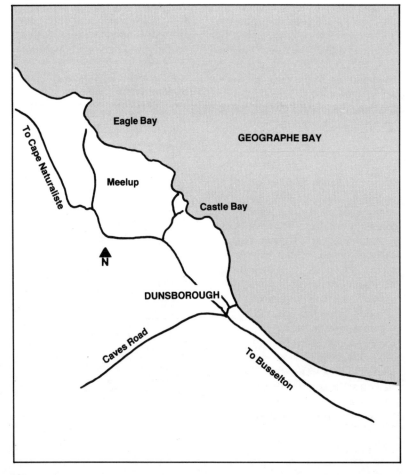

quiet water is perfect for young children. Older children and adults who like a little more action in their water, will find moderate surf in Castle Rock Bay and Eagle Bay, next around the headland.

For boat owners the news is not so good, for the shallow water that is ideal for children is less than ideal for launching boats. Indeed only boats which can be dragged across the beach are really suitable here. Sailboards, catamarans and small fishing boats will have no trouble, but larger craft will find launching difficult, even with a four-wheel drive vehicle. The best idea is to haul the boats up to Busselton, only a few kilometres away, and launch them there.

Fishing is superb from the beach, the rocks, or a boat. And in the shallow water off Dunsborough Beach you can even hand-spear fish at night. All kinds of sailing are easy in the quiet water and skindiving is

excellent around the bluffs and coves of Cape Naturaliste. As mentioned, there is a moderate surf on the small beaches in the coves, but if surfing is your sport, then you should drive the eight kilometres over the headland to Yallingup Beach where there is one of the most popular surfing spots on the West Coast.

Dunsborough is the jump-off point for a whole variety of interesting activities. Just along the Yallingup road is an animal park, while the drive out to the Cape Naturaliste lighthouse provides some magnificent coastal panoramas. There is a country club with bowls, golf and tennis and the little shopping centre is extremely well-equipped to meet any needs. There are beach huts to rent if you wish, and a first-class caravan park located right on the beach. Much of the area falls within the Leeuwin-Naturaliste National Park, so

By road   250km S of Perth
RAC Depot   See Busselton
Caravan access   Sealed road all the way
Best weather   November thru' February
Accommodation   1 hotel, 2 caravan parks
Beaches   Dunsborough Beach, Castle Bay, Eagle Bay
Rock fishing   Excellent
Beach fishing   Excellent
Offshore fishing   Excellent, but launching may be difficult
Still water fishing   Limited
Sailing   Excellent
Sailboarding   Excellent
Trailer-sailers   Good, but launching may be difficult
Water skiing   Excellent
Canoeing   Excellent
Skindiving   Excellent
Fuel and Bait   Local store
Boat hire   None
Ramps   Over-beach at Dunsborough
National Parks   Leeuwin-Naturaliste
Interests   Superb scenery around Cape Naturaliste. Site of old whaling station. Wildlife park

bushwalking is an added interest.

Together with its adjoining centres of Meelup and Eagle Bay, Dunsborough is a fine spot in which to spend a family holiday.

Delightful sandy coves fringe the western shores of Geographe Bay

YALLINGUP

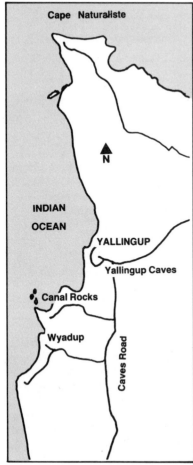

Yallingup is unquestionably one of the most spectacular beaches in this south-western region. Even on a quiet day huge surf waves pound into the crescent-shaped bay. It is a very popular beach with surfers and according to the experts, provides some fine boardriding. This, of course, limits its appeal mostly to surfers and those who like surf swimming. It is much too rough for children, although at the southern end of the beach, the big waves are broken by a rock shelf and the water is relatively quiet.

The village is divided into two with the Yallingup Caves section about a kilometre up the road on top of the hill. There is a camping ground and a store here, but most of the facilities are down at the beach.

These include another store and a few other shops. Accommodation at the beach is in a caravan park although there is a modern resort building with holiday units and a few guest houses.

The southern part of the bay sweeps round to another settlement known as Smiths Beach. This has a caravan park but little else, as has Canal Rocks, named after a row of rocks which protrude well out into the sea. Smiths Beach is a surf beach as is the next indented cove at Wyadup. Surfing is the name of the game here, certainly as far as water activities is concerned.

Boating is impossible for these bays all face the tempestuous Southern Ocean. There is no constructed ramp although it is possible to launch over the beach in some quieter corners. But small boats would not be safe in the big seas immediately off the beach, so if offshore fishing is your sport, then tow your boat to Busselton and launch in quieter water.

Similarly, most other water sports are difficult at Yallingup. Wave-riding with a sailboard would be possible although you would need to be an expert because the surf is very steep. But small boat or catamaran sailing would be asking for trouble both in terms of damage to the boat and injury to the crew. Skindiving is excellent for the water is very clear, but once again, launching a boat would be a problem. You may have to settle for skindiving around the headlands or else take the boat to Busselton.

Away from the water there are plenty of alternative activities. Being mostly national park, the headlands around Cape Naturaliste offer excellent bushwalks. If walking is not your scene then drive the car out to the Cape lighthouse and enjoy some magnificent coastal scenery. The Yallingup Caves are just at the top of the hill, and these are well worth a visit, while for the youngsters, a visit to Bannamah wildlife park is always a popular choice.

Superb coastal scenery is a feature of this area, so even if you do not plan to surf the beaches, take a run to Canal Rocks, Smiths Beach and Wyadup. There are few more spectacular spots along the coastline.

By road	265km S of Perth
RAC Depot	See Busselton
Caravan access	Sealed road all the way
Best weather	November thru' February
Accommodation	3 caravan parks, 1 hotel
Beaches	Yallingup Beach, Smiths Beach, Wyadup
Rock fishing	Excellent
Beach fishing	Excellent
Offshore fishing	Excellent, but very difficult launching
Still water fishing	None
Sailing	Limited, open sea only
Sailboarding	Good, open sea only
Trailer-sailers	Not suitable
Water skiing	Not suitable
Canoeing	Not suitable
Skindiving	Excellent
Fuel and Bait	Local store
Boat hire	None
Ramps	None
National Parks	Leeuwin-Naturaliste
Interests	Good surf beaches. Yallingup Caves

GRACETOWN

Although the small, rock-strewn bay on which Gracetown is located is quite attractive, the settlement itself does not in any way do justice to its name. Tier upon tier of mostly fibro-box cottages climb up the hillside with their television aerials and power and telephone poles looking like the remains of a burned-out forest. It seems a shame that in such a pleasant setting a little more forethought and planning was not applied.

Nevertheless, the bay is pretty and has a variety of activities to offer. It is particularly suited to families with small children for the big Southern Ocean swells outside are broken by the headlands, and the waves that roll onto the beach

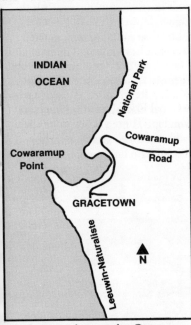

are almost only a ripple. Quite a contrast with many of the other bays along this coast which are renowned for their good surf waves.

The small sheltered beach in the northern corner of the bay is particularly attractive and has a white sand beach with sparkling clear water. This beach is also used for boat launching, but there is no constructed ramp, so only boats towed by four-wheel drive vehicles can launch there. Once launched, however, boats have an easy passgae to the outside water, for although there is a heavy break on each of the headlands, the water in the middle of the bay is smooth.

Skindiving is a favourite sport at Gracetown for not only is the water crystal clear, but there are interesting reefs and islands offshore where fish and other treasures abound. Getting a boat out is easy compared to many of the other bays, so skindivers are among the groups who find Gracetown an ideal spot for their sport. Bushwalking is popular, too, for there are many walks through the coastal heath vegetation, much of which falls within the Leeuwin-Naturaliste National Park.

There is no caravan park at Gracetown, nor any other form of accommodation other than holiday units. One store takes care of all the holiday needs, although Margaret River is not all that far away. There is a caravan park at the turnoff from the highway and this is the nearest accommodation available although it is some distance from the beach.

The hinterland behind the beaches is magnificent. Green hills and stately forests intermingle to present a delightful passing scene when driving along Caves Road. This is the wine-growing area of the south-west and every second property is a vineyard. Since the lush green of the vines always create a pleasant sight, they enhance the

natural beauty of the area and make a drive down this coast road a delightful exercise.

Likewise the coastal scenery, which is spectacular. From the hill above Gracetown, the view northwards resembles a scene from the West Coast of Ireland with ruggedly beautiful headlands following one after the other and all clothed in the white mist of the breaking surf. Since this coast has been battered for untold centuries by the combined fury of the Southern and Indian Oceans, it is small wonder that it has been carved into such dramatic beauty. The weathered rocks, surmounted by the clinging coastal heath form the main bastion of the Australian continents's defence against the ceaseless erosion of the oceans.

The village of Gracetown may not live up to its name, but the beauty of the surrounding coastline more than makes up for it.

By road 270 km S of Perth
RAC depot See Margaret River
Caravan access Good road in from highway
Best weather November thru' February
Accommodation Cowamarup caravan park
Beaches Town beach and adjacent bays
Rock fishing Excellent
Beach fishing Excellent
Offshore fishing Excellent, but launching difficult
Still water fishing None
Sailing Limited, open sea only
Sailboarding Good
Trailer-sailers Launching too difficult
Water-skiing Limited
Canoeing Limited, open sea only
Skindiving Excellent on offshore reefs
Fuel and bait Local store
Boat hire None
Ramps Over beach only
National parks Leeuwin-Naturaliste NP
Interests Bushwalking. Interesting coastal scenery

MARGARET RIVER

Far to the south of Australia, in latitudes known as the 'Roaring Forties', the winds tear around the world in an endless series of gales. Whipped up by these gales, the seas are driven at breakneck speed, tumbling over themselves as they build to mammoth proportions. The Antarctic ice pack adds its contribution to what amounts to the world's most inhospitable climate. Fortunately the worst of this climate stays well south near the ice, but the southernmost capes of the world's land masses catch the fringes of this fury and become areas of awesome climatic conditions, dreaded by sailors and settlers alike.

The south-western tip of Australia does not protrude far enough south to even catch the fringe of this foul weather, but the prevailing south-westerly winds carry some of the perpetual rain up over the ocean and deposit it on the land. The rain, combined with the temperate climate, produce lush growth and over the centuries giant forests have developed in the south-west of the continent. Huge Jarrah and Karri stands astounded

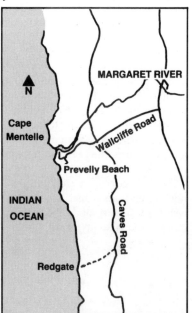

and frustrated the early settlers and gave rise to the first major industry in this part of Australia—timber getting.

But a more viable rural industry was necessary to enable the continent to grow, which meant that land had to be cleared of the forests and crops sown. To encourage such development, a Group Settlement Scheme was established in the 1920s to encourage migrants to the country regions of the south-west and extend the land development. In 1922, some 100 settlers arrived on the banks of the Margaret River and established the township which now bears that name. From the lush forests, these pioneers developed the dairy industry which established the region as a viable agricultural area.

Nowadays the undulating green countryside of the Margaret River produces a wide variety of rural products, one of the most recent and most important of which is wine. Together with tourism, the vineyards account for a rapid rise in the popularity of this delightful country town and its surrounding areas, for if ever a centre were ideally suited to both industries, Margaret River is that centre. While the excellent climatic conditions and good soil produce fine grapes, the historic little town itself, together with its nearby coastal resorts, creates a perfect environment for transient visitors or for family holidays.

Here you can enjoy the best of two worlds. If the water takes your fancy, then there are magnificent beaches at Prevelly Park, near the mouth of the Margaret River, Gnarabup Beach and Redgate. If you are more interested in the vineyards, then take a tour of the hinterland which boasts over 400 hectares of vine plantations. There are quaint family vineyards, established on only a few hectares of

ground, and there are major commercial establishments with plantings covering more than 100 hectares. Both welcome visitors, although a check with the Tourist Bureau is recommended to find out which vineyards are open and when.

There are a number of other features of interest in the area which will particularly appeal to tourists, not least of which are the nearby caves. The coast road is known as the Caves Road since it provides access to a number of interesting caves, one of which has a display of fossils of prehistoric animals including a fossil of the now presumed-extinct Tasmanian Tiger. Fine old buildings such as Wallcliffe House, built in 1865, dot the area, while the wildflowers and wildlife of the south-west are to be seen at their very best in this area. The coastal strip from Cape Naturaliste to Cape Leeuwin is almost entirely preserved as a wonderful national park. It is in this park that the wildflowers and fauna are at their best.

For families on holiday, the coastal strip holds much more

By road 280km S of Perth
RAC Depot See Augusta or Busselton
Caravan access Sealed road all the way
Best weather November thru' February
Accommodation 1 motel, 1 hotel/motel, 4 caravan parks
Beaches Prevelly Park, Redgate, Cowaramup
Rock fishing Excellent
Beach fishing Excellent
Offshore fishing Excellent, but launching may be difficult
Still water fishing Limited in river and estuary
Sailing Limited in estuary
Sailboarding Good, open sea only
Trailer-sailers Not suitable
Water skiing Not suitable
Canoeing Excellent in river
Skindiving Excellent along coast
Fuel and Bait Local stores
Boat hire None
Ramps Cowaramup
National Parks Leeuwin-Naturaliste
Interests Vineyards. Caves. Superb coastline

A unique semi-circular surf wave breaks round the reef at Prevelly Park

interest than just the national park. It is a very spectacular coast for its entire length and is indented with magnificent surf and swimming beaches. One of the best is at Prevelly Park, near the mouth of the Margaret River. Here there is fine surfing indeed, for a reef off the headland creates a wide, sweeping curve of wave that will delight the heart of any boardrider, to say nothing of rock fishermen. Much of the beach is pounded by surf, but there are quiet areas where children can swim with reasonable safety.

Because of the surf, other boating activities are somewhat limited. Certainly launching a boat of any size is out of the question, and sailing close to the headlands or beaches would be dangerous. Wave-

sailing, by contrast, is well suited to the surf break here, and is almost as popular a sport as surfing. Launching fishing boats of any size is also limited by the sea conditions although there are ramps at Gnarabup and Cowaramup. Beach fishing is the major sport, and these beaches are ideally suited to the sport. For those who prefer quieter water, the mouth of the Margaret River provides a good venue where it laps the sandbar which separates it from the ocean.

The area along this coast is essentially an area for outdoor activities. There is not much in the way of entertainment other than some nice restaurants in the town of Margaret River. Accommodation is also somewhat restricted to camping

and caravan parks, particularly along the coast. There is one hotel and one motel in the town and a few guesthouses to supplement the caravan parks. But in such delightful countryside, surely the way to live is in the big outdoors, especially along the coast where most of the caravan parks and camping grounds are located in superb natural areas.

Margaret River and its surrounding region is a delightful spot to visit, either while touring the coast, or for a relaxing, away-from-it-all holiday. Apart from its lovely coastal environment, the Leeuwin-Naturaliste National Park, and its pleasant township, it has more features of interest and more attractive countryside than most holiday areas in this part of the world.

HAMELIN BAY

The tiny village of Hamelin WA has no connection with its namesake in Europe or the pied piper that brought that town its fame. However, the pied piper

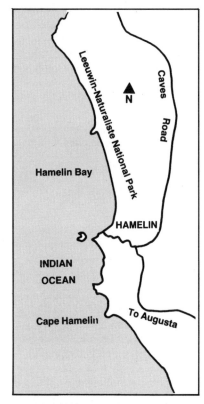

could have done worse than to lead his children to the 'down-under' Hamelin for this tiny coastal resort on the south-west tip of Australia is tailor-made for children. No matter what age, there is something for every child here, despite the fact that there is only one shop that sells ice-creams!

For those who can handle the surf, there are varying degrees and sizes of waves across the face of Hamelin Bay. Near the village the big swells of the Southern Ocean are tamed by the offshore island and rocks as well as the sandy headland, so that in the very corner of the Bay, where the village is located, there is flat tranquil water. And not only flat, but also as clear as glass, for there are no polluting cities or even silt-carrying rivers to cloud the crystal-clear waters of Hamelin Bay.

Despite its size—there is only a handful of houses—Hamelin has a very rich history, for once it was one of the principal ports along the West Australian coast, and hundreds of thousands of tonnes of timber were loaded aboard windjammers lying out in the Bay. To this day the remains of the old jetty stand as a nostalgic relic of those halcyon days. The only trade that exists in Hamelin now is the fishing, and that is limited to but a few small craft.

Scenically it is a beautiful bay, with a wide, silver sand beach sweeping away to the north to terminate in one of the craggy headlands that are a feature of this coast. The village is snugged up under the low sandstone bluff at the southern end with a sizeable island offshore creating a good breakwater. The water in this corner of the Bay is surprisingly shallow, and since it is so crystal clear, every feature of the sea bed is clearly visible. Skindivers must find this area an absolute paradise, for apart from the fish, shells and other treasures to be

found in these waters, there is always the possibility of a real treasure trove find in the form of a relic from one of the old ships.

Nearby Cape Leeuwin lighthouse is an important mariner's signpost, for ships travelling across the Southern Ocean pick up this light as their first landfall on the Australian continent. The name was given to the Cape by the early Dutch explorers and literally translated means

'lioness'. The lighthouse is accessible through nearby Augusta, and the bush that covers its storm-wracked headlands is protected by one of Western Australia's finest national parks—the Leeuwin-Naturaliste National Park. Bushwalking in this area is a delight, particularly in springtime when the wildflowers are in abundance.

Fishing comes in every form at Hamelin. The surf fishing along the beach is second to none, and rock fishing from the headlands is good, although the clear, shallow water makes the fish shy on sunny days. The ramp is a solid wood structure and all sizes and shapes of boats can be launched over it, although at low tide the water at the bottom of the ramp is shallow, and large boats may need to wait until the tide rises to avoid getting their transom stuck in the sand.

The trip out to Hamelin is a long drive, and the accommodation limited to one small caravan park. But the superb scenery and the magic water makes it all so very worth while. And, of course, long distances tend to keep the crowds away, which is always an attraction if you like your holidays to be reasonably quiet and peaceful. For such a holiday I can thoroughly recommend Hamelin.

Launching a boat beside the remains of Hamelin Bay's historic old jetty

AUGUSTA

Although the discovery and exploration of Australia is commonly related to Captain Cook and the east coast of the continent, in fact the west coast received attention from explorers and navigators more than a century before Cook even entered the Southern Hemisphere. Dutch adventurers Hartog, Houtman and Jacobsz made exploratory forays along the west coast of Australia in the years before 1620. More than a century before Cook reached the coast of New South Wales, virtually the whole of the western, northern and part of the southern shores of the continent had been explored and in some cases charted.

On 6 December 1801 master navigator Matthew Flinders sighted Cape Leeuwin and began his survey of the southern coast which resulted eventually in his total circumnavigation of the continent. This epic charting voyage is commemorated by a memorial which stands on the coast near Cape Leeuwin and the small inlet which bears his name—Flinders Bay. Here, some thirty years later, settlers came ashore to open up the heavily timbered forest behind the coast and establish the small but busy town of Augusta.

They built their town on the estuary of the Blackwood River—a location which makes it ideal as a holiday centre. On the one side of the estuary is the promontory of Cape Leeuwin with its rugged, but attractive coastal scenery, and on the other is an unlimited stretch of surf beach backed by high sand hills. The estuary itself forms Hardy Inlet, a quiet stretch of water with pleasant sandy beaches near the entrance and reed-lined shores

By road   316km SW of Perth
RAC Depot   Nutley's Garage, Phone 58 1515, 58 1854
Caravan access   Sealed road all the way
Best weather   November thru' February
Accommodation   1 hotel/motel, 4 caravan parks
Beaches   Flinders Bay
Rock fishing   Excellent
Beach fishing   Excellent
Offshore fishing   Excellent but access over dangerous bar
Still water fishing   Excellent in Blackwood River and Estuary
Sailing   Excellent in Hardy Inlet
Sailboarding   Excellent in Inlet or open sea
Trailer-sailers   Good in Inlet
Water skiing   Good in Inlet
Canoeing   Excellent in River and Inlet
Skindiving   Excellent along coast
Fuel and Bait   Town stores
Boat hire   Charter cruises at town jetty
Ramps   Flinders Bay. Township foreshores
National Parks   Scott N P, Leeuwin-Naturaliste N P
Interests   Cape Leeuwin lighthouse and waterwheel. Wildflowers. Wildfowl in Hardys Inlet. Superb coastal scenery

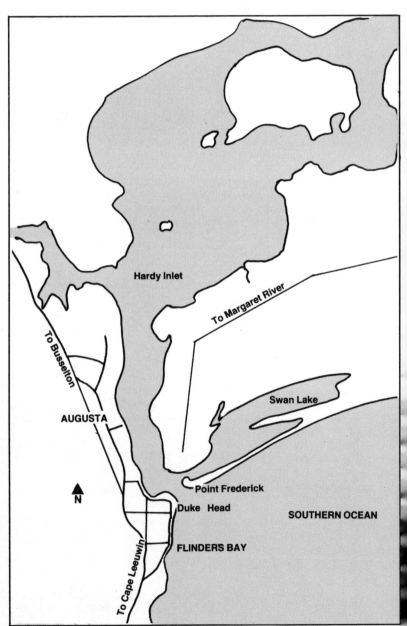

farther upstream where it becomes the Blackwood River, meandering back into the timbered inland of the south-west region of Western Australia.

Such a setting means lots of water activities, and what better suits summer holidays than water activities. In Augusta there is almost every type of water suited to almost every type of water activity. Flinders Bay is open to the Southern Ocean and therefore has moderate surf on its beaches, although in the far southern corner there are quiet spots where children can enjoy relatively still water. For those who prefer much quieter water, however, the shores of the estuary are ideal with no surf whatsoever but clean, blue water which makes for good swimming. The open beaches provide good sport for boardriders and wave-sailing enthusiasts although the surf never gets as high as it does on some of the beaches to the north.

Quiet-water sailing can be found anywhere from Flinders Bay up the inlet and into the river. Sailboarders and canoeists will particularly enjoy this stretch of water, for although larger boats such as trailer-sailers can launch here, there are some shallow banks in parts of the Inlet and these will inhibit sailing for all but shallow-draft vessels. Fishing boats can make out through the entrance to the open sea, but the bar can be dangerous and boatowners without experience should take great care. Local fishermen are always ready to assist if asked, and their advice should be sought if you are intending to make out to sea. Fishing in the Inlet is reputed to be good, and this can be done from the river banks, from the shore or from a boat.

Fishing along the coast is also good, with rock and beach fishing the most popular methods of wetting a line. Marroning, that uniquely Western Australian sport, is also available in the fresh water rivers of the area. The season is from 15 December to 1 May and a license must be obtained to take the succulent shellfish. Diving is also popular in the clear waters off the coast, and there are many reefs and underwater gutters off the rugged headlands which are the haunt of big fish and lobster.

Away from the water, there are a number of interesting features in the region. The town itself is compact, built on the slopes of the hillsides overlooking Hardys Inlet. It is well set up for holiday requirements, including accommodation in a number of different forms. The road out to Cape Leeuwin offers a magnificent scenic drive, as does the Caves Road, running north to Yallingup. As its name denotes, this road passes a number of interesting caves, some of which are described in this book under the heading of Margaret River. Cape Leeuwin lighthouse is open on Tuesday and Thursday mornings, although the grounds are open every day. An old waterwheel, constructed in 1895 to provide water for the men building the lighthouse, has become encrusted with mineral salts to the point that it appears to be carved from stone.

These are but a few of the interesting features in the vicinity of Augusta. There is so much to see and do in this quiet southern town that the only way to discover them all is to stay a while and explore the area.

Boating is available on either sheltered or open water at Augusta

WINDY HARBOUR

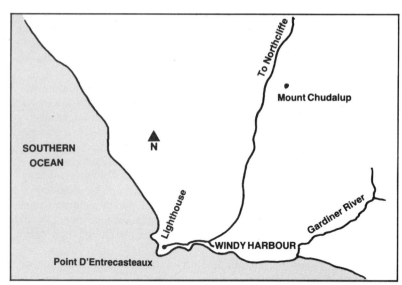

By road   400km S of Perth
RAC Depot   Shell Service Station, Northcliffe. Phone76 7021, 76 7032
Caravan access   Sealed road all the way
Best weather   November thru' February
Accommodation   1 caravan park
Beaches   Windy Harbour Beach
Rock fishing   Excellent
Beach fishing   Excellent
Offshore fishing   Excellent, but launching may be difficult
Still water fishing   None
Sailing   Limited, open sea only
Sailboarding   Good, open sea only
Trailer-sailers   Not suitable
Water skiing   Not suitable
Canoeing   Limited, open sea only
Skindiving   Excellent around coast and islands
Fuel and Bait   Northcliffe
Boat hire   None
Ramps   Over-beach only
National Parks   Mt Chudalup N P
Interests   Mt Chudalup. Cape D'Entrecasteaux. Lighthouse

The name Windy Harbour is a contradiction in terms for there would seem little point in chosing a harbour that is windy. Harbours are meant for shelter. But however much of a contradiction in terms it may be, Windy Harbour certainly

Windy Harbour lives up to its name

lives up to its name. Although snugged up under the lee of massive Point D'Entrecasteaux, it is a wide, open bay facing south to the raging turmoil of the Roaring Forties and the huge seas that build up in that unpleasant area.

The bay has no shelter at all, although the swells are broken by

rocks in the western corner and thus provide a little relief from the surf which breaks along most of the beach. At the time of my survey a howling southerly was blowing. The seas were whipped up to a

The south west is renowned for its wildflowers

frenzy and the smattering of fishing boats in the bay strained and tugged at their moorings and wallowed frantically in the steep waves. Even the tops of the sand dunes were blown off, creating a blizzard of stinging sand particles. Windy Harbour indeed!

Having said that, however, now let's look on the credit side. The beaches, when not blown around, are beautiful. Backed by low sand hills, the main surf beach stretches away to the east and south, a wide crescent of soft sand with usually sufficient surf to gladden a board-rider's heart. In the western corner, as mentioned, the swell is broken by a gaggle of rocks and there is relatively quiet water here. This is the spot for youngsters and it is also the spot for boat launching. There are two so-called ramps at Windy Harbour; one near the ranger's house, which leads directly over the beach, and the one in the western corner which leads to

relatively quiet water. Both, however, need four-wheel drive vehicles for launching.

Accommodation at Windy Harbour is either in the caravan park or in a strange 'village' of huts, the like of which are rarely seen these days. In years gone by many of the small, inaccessible coastal spots became haunts of 'squatters' who erected shanty towns where they could while away the holiday hours unworried by officialdom and restrictive licensing. The gaggle of huts at Windy Harbour, although reasonably well constructed, still have that shanty-town appearance. It could almost be a film set for an old gold-mining movie!

The camping ground is set among the bush behind the sand dunes and there is a ranger on-site. A road from the village leads to magnificent Cape D'Entrecasteaux, a striking bluff with its lighthouse stuck incongruously on the top. The immediate hinterland is coastal

heath which makes for fascinating walking trips and is alive with wildlife—particularly tortoises. A few kilometres along the road to Northcliffe, the nearest shopping centre, is the incredible bulk of Mount Chudalup, a bald, grey monolith rock, not unlike Ayers Rock in shape, towering up out of the forest like a huge whale surfacing through the waves. It is concealed when driving in from Northcliffe, but on the way back it creates a most striking visual impact.

Most water sports can be enjoyed in the pleasant surroundings of Windy Harbour, although small boating activity will be curtailed if the sea is up or the wind blowing. Surfing, sailboarding and swimming are the most popular. Beach and rock fishing are good and skindiving is superb. Despite its name and the exposed nature of the bay which creates the problem, Windy Harbour has a lot going for it and makes for a pleasant spot to visit, perhaps even to stay.

WALPOLE

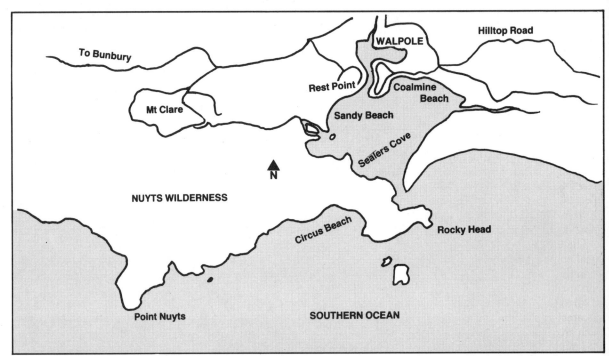

The southern tip of south-west Australia forms a rugged battlement which resists the ceaseless onslaught of the Southern Ocean. Over the centuries, the sea has worn back many of the coast's more vulnerable defences, driving deep indentations between the areas where the land has held firm. As a result, the coastline of this southern bastion has been eroded into a saw-toothed irregularity with massive bald granite headlands protruding defiantly into the ocean and deep, beach-fringed indentations retreating back into the hinterland. In some cases, the invading sea breaks through these rearguard beaches and floods the low-lying coastal land behind, forming deep inlets with wide stretches of placid, almost land-locked water.

Because of their location behind the sandhills of the coast, and the tranquil nature of the countryside through which they roam, these inlets are picturesque and attractive. One of the most attractive is Nornalup Inlet, now the centre of a beautiful national park. Set behind a massive barrier of secondary sand dunes, and protected by a solid granite headland, Nornalup Inlet and its associated Walpole Inlet create a delightful stretch of sheltered water. Together with their surrounding national park, the inlets form a perfect location for all kinds of recreational and tourist activities and are rapidly becoming one of the focal points of tourism in the south-west.

The offerings of this magnificent natural area are almost too extensive to detail in a book of this kind. Day visitors and passing tourists will be hard-pressed to take in all there is to see, and unquestionably this is a spot to stay for a while so that nothing is missed. Just the coastal scenery alone is worth an extended visit, for it ranges from long, wide stretches of clean, untrammeled beach, to rugged mountains falling in steep gradients to rocky coves and inlets. The names alone stir a sense of adventure, for who could resist exploring the secrets behind the name Hush-Hush Beach, or why Lost Beach is so-called, to say nothing of what the imagination could do with Circus Beach!

Then there is Crystal Lake, Boggy Lake, Conspicuous Cliff, the Peppermints, Snake Ledge and

By road 424km S of Perth
RAC Depot See Denmark
Caravan access Sealed road to all points
Best weather November thru' February
Accommodation 1 hotel/motel, 1 guest house, 2 caravan parks
Beaches Coalmine Beach. Mandalay Beach. Sandy Beach
Rock fishing Excellent
Beach fishing Excellent
Offshore fishing Excellent
Still water fishing Excellent
Sailing Excellent in Nornalup and Walpole Inlets
Sailboarding Excellent
Trailer-sailers Good. Launching may be limited by size of craft
Water skiing Excellent
Canoeing Excellent
Skindiving Excellent along coast
Fuel and Bait Town stores
Boat hire None
Ramps Coalmine Beach. Rest Point
National Parks Walpole-Nornalup N P
Interests Nuyts Wilderness. Conspicuous Cliff. Hilltop Road. Wildflowers

Sealers Cove, to mention only a few more. Exploring the origin of these names is as interesting as exploring the places themselves. Many of the early explorers and settlers lost their sense of the romantic when they named their discoveries, opting mostly for the names of civic dignitaries or prominent citizens. Like Matthew Flinders, the early settlers who gave these delightful names to the features around Nornalup Inlet were far more inspired and used their imagination and their sense of the romantic rather than honouring some dusty old dignitary.

The township of Walpole is the focal point of the area, located as it is on the main southern highway and at the head of the inlets. It is a small town, but quite well equipped to cater for tourists and vacationers, with an adequate shopping centre and moderate accommodation in the form of a hotel/motel and two guest houses. There are two caravan parks, one on either side of the narrow channel which separates the inlets. This is not really sufficient accommodation for the number of visitors that arrive each summer, so in peak seasons it is wise to book ahead.

The main coastal area of the Walpole-Nornalup National Park is divided by the inlet itself. On the western side there is the superb Nuyts Wilderness region, with access only on foot, where nature is undisturbed and fine stands of Karri, among other native species, are to be found. Across the narrow straits are the extensive secondary sand dunes of the Nornalup area which extend eastwards to Point Irwin and Peaceful Bay, through forests of Red Flowering Gum. Access to this area by car is easier, there being a good road down to the beach under Conspicuous Cliff, and four-wheel vehicle access to The Gap and Herring Rock. There are numerous lookouts and vantage points along the access roads providing panoramas of the surrounding countryside.

Boatowners will find the Walpole area close to Paradise. The extensive inlet has good fishing, being a nursery for many offshore species of fish. Access to sea is possible through the entrance, and the fishing in these Southern Ocean waters is highly regarded by the experts. However, the Southern Ocean, like any ocean, is potentially dangerous, and only experi-

enced boatowners with seaworthy craft should attempt to make out through the Heads. For non-fishing boatowners, the scenic delights of the inlets are there for the taking, and there are many small beaches on which to pull up the boat and enjoy a picnic in delightful natural surroundings. Beach and rock fishermen are also well catered for, although they will need to take one of the tracks down to the coast, or the road out to Mandalay Beach.

Swimming, surfing and wave-sailing is best at Mandalay Beach, while small-boat sailors, sailboarders and catamaran enthusiasts need look no farther than the inlet itself which, although it has a few shoal patches, is tailor-made for all still-water activities. There are boat ramps at points around the shoreline, mostly near the caravan parks, and still-water beaches for small children along the Coalmine Beach and Nornalup shores. Add to this the delights of the wildflowers and native fauna, all protected by the national park, and you have a prime reason why a visit to Walpole is well worth the trip south. It is also a good reason to make your stay a fairly lengthy one.

Coalmine Beach, one of many sheltered spots in Nornalup Inlet

PEACEFUL BAY

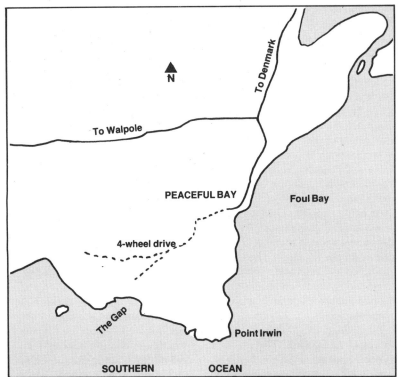

By road Approx 415km S of Perth
RAC Depot See Denmark
Caravan access Good gravel road (10km) from higway turnoff
Best weather November thru' February
Accommodation 1 caravan park
Beaches Peaceful Bay
Rock fishing Good
Beach fishing Excellent
Offshore fishing Excellent, but launching may be difficult
Still water fishing None
Sailing Limited, open sea only
Sailboarding Good, open sea only
Trailer-sailers Not suitable
Water skiing Not suitable
Canoeing Limited, open sea only
Skindiving Excellent on offshore reefs
Fuel and Bait Local stores
Boat hire None
Ramps Over-beach only
National Parks Walpole-Nornalup N P
Interests Coastal scenery and bushwalking

One might well wonder if some of the early explorers or settlers were totally serious when naming some of the bays and harbours around the coast of Western Australia. First there was Windy Harbour now Peaceful Bay. So what is wrong with Peaceful Bay you may ask? The answer is that there is nothing wrong with Peaceful Bay as a name,

Peaceful Bay is deserving of its name

except that it is part of a larger bay called, believe it or not, Foul Bay!

Whatever the cause of the confusion, there is no question which is the more suitable name. The bay in question is peaceful, calm and picturesque, and even when the sea and weather are foul in Foul Bay, all is peaceful in Peaceful Bay! The reason is that Peaceful Bay is snugged close under a headland which gives it shelter from the prevailing

southerlies or westerlies and breaks the big Southern Ocean swell down to a mere ripple. To reduce the swell even further, the corner of the Bay is almost surrounded by offlying rocks creating a totally natural harbour, almost a lagoon in the style of coral atolls.

This means it is a perfect spot for boating and swimming, although to get a boat into the water you need a four-wheel drive vehicle, for the ramp, like all the ramps along this coast, runs over the beach. This is a pity because in such a great natural harbour, a good concrete ramp would enable many more craft to take to the water, particularly large fishing boats and trailer-sailers.

From a scenic point of view, Peaceful Bay is a sheer delight, its white crescent of sand sweeping north around the Bay and the smooth, round granite rocks resembling whales surfacing just off the shore. The entrance is narrow but deep so boat access is easy and the water is a beautiful turquoise with shadowy features on the bottom showing through as dark patches. Behind the beach, the dunes form a prominent barrier with sea grass on the foreshores and coastal scrub in the hinterland.

William Bay can be only described as sheer visual impact. It is one of the finest bays on this part of the coast with spectacular geographical formations of the like rarely seen anywhere on the Australian coastline. Perhaps one way to describe it is a coastal region where a giant has scattered his marbles indiscriminately along the shore and into the sea. Children will know exactly what I mean as will adults who were brought up with the legends of giants and trolls.

The spectacle begins as you drive through the delightful bush of the William Bay National Park. This in itself is a visual feast, especially in spring when the wildflowers carpet the coastal hills. Some of these hills have strange structures on their peaks—a group of smoothed, often rounded boulders, seemingly placed there by some giant's hand. The illusion becomes reality as more of these hills appear and the master-piece is the final hill before the coast falls away to the sea. A huge sand hill, probably 70 metres high, crowned by a cluster of huge pointed boulders, as near to resembling a

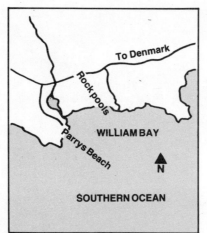

crown as a fairytale giant could make it.

Then comes the second surprise. The beach, which stretches away to the south, is scattered with more boulders. Small ones, large ones, huge ones, giving the effect exactly as I described of giant marbles scattered indiscriminately along the beach and into the water. It really is a breathtaking spectacle, yet it does not mar the beach, for there is plenty of room for sand between rocks, many of which are sunk well in. Indeed, the cluster of rocks in the southern corner of the beach break down the ocean swell to almost millpond conditions and create a huge natural swimming pool with rocks all round and a sandy bottom. This pool is called

The unique Children's Pool, one of many natural delights in William Bay

the 'Childrens' Pool', and that really says it all.

There are other scenic delights in the area but none to match William Bay. Since it is a national park, there is no accommodation, but there is a sealed road all the way in and an excellent car park with public toilets. Apart from drinking in the scenic delight, you can swim, fish or walk, or, for that matter, just soak up the sun. You will not find better surroundings in which to do any of those things for many a mile along this coast.

Boats are out although you can carry a board down the steps to the beach. But nearby Parrys Beach has access for boats near the camping ground, although you will need a four-wheel drive vehicle to get the boat over the sand. Parrys Beach is a popular surf beach and it also has some fairly spectacular scenery in the high hills that rear up over the beach. Eroded sandstone has formed into pitted caves on the steep hillside, leaving many rock faces looking alarmingly unstable.

There is not much at Parrys Beach other than a caravan park and camping ground. The road winds over the hill to the next bay but it is rough and conventional vehicles are likely to get bogged down. Between them, however, William Bay and Parrys Beach offer two distinctly different coastal features within a few kilometres of each other.

By road 430km SE of Perth
RAC Depot See Denmark
Caravan access Sealed road to William Bay. Gravel to Parrys Beach
Best weather November thru' March
Accommodation None
Beaches William Bay. Madfish Bay. Parrys Beach
Rock fishing Excellent
Beach fishing Excellent
Offshore fishing Excellent, but launching may be difficult
Still water fishing Limited
Sailing Limited, open sea only (Parrys Beach)
Sailboarding Good, open sea only
Trailer-sailers Not suitable
Water skiing Not suitable
Canoeing Limited
Skindiving Excellent
Fuel and Bait See Denmark
Boat hire None
Ramps Over-beach only at Parrys Beach
National Parks William Bay N P
Interests Superb coastal scenery in William Bay National Park. Rock Pools

DENMARK

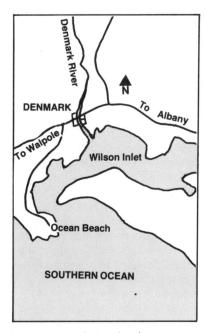

Massive sandhills form the coastline east of Wilson Inlet

There is no relationship between the name of this town and its counterpart in Europe. The tidy little town in the south-west of Western Australia was named by an early visitor, Dr Thomas Braidwood Wilson, who was temporarily stranded in the area while his ship was being repaired on a passage to New South Wales. He named the area after his friend and colleague, Surgeon Denmark, RN. Coincidentally, the good doctor was himself to be the recipient of a similar honour when, in later years, the NSW town of Braidwood was named after him.

Denmark grew very slowly through the pioneering years. The heavy stands of forest that are common to the south-west inhibited much rural development, and for years the only product of consequence that left Denmark was the Karri which was so prized by timber-users all over the world. When a mill was built in 1895 the settlement was established, and before many years had passed, the Karri from Denmark was being used as paving blocks for the streets of London,

and telegraph poles, railway sleepers and wharf piles in such diversified countries as China, Africa and South America. Clearing the forests gave the farmers a chance to till the soil, and agricultural products soon joined the timber shipped out of this small, but thriving community.

The Group Settlement Scheme, described in the Margaret River section of this book, gave the area an added impetus when it was introduced in 1922, but the 1930s Depression that followed, proved an unpleasant setback. Since then a few timber mills have come and gone, and the rural sector has consolidated its beef and pork production, but otherwise there have been no major developments of any consequence in the little town. At least, not until tourism moved in. Recent years have seen an upsurge of quite remarkable proportions in this new industry which has become a prime factor in Denmark's commercial life.

It should come as no surprise to know that this southern town is a

popular tourist venue, for the coastal region is one of the most striking in the whole of Australia, and the hinterland forests are renown for their beauty. Apart from the magnificent Jarrah, Karri and Tingle

By road 466km SE of Perth
RAC Depot Valria Auto Spares and Repairs, Phone 48 1288
Caravan access Sealed road to all points
Best weather November thru' February
Accommodation 2 motels, 1 hotel/motel, 1 guest house, 3 caravan parks
Beaches Ocean Beach
Rock fishing Excellent
Beach fishing Excellent
Offshore fishing Good, but access difficult
Still water fishing Excellent in Wilson Inlet
Sailing Excellent in Inlet
Sailboarding Excellent
Trailer-sailers Good in Inlet
Water skiing Excellent in Inlet
Canoeing Excellent in Inlet
Skindiving Excellent along coastal headlands
Fuel and Bait Town stores
Boat hire None
Ramps At points around Wilson Inlet
National Parks William Bay N P
Interests Valley of the Giants. Wildflowers

trees which are so unique to this part of the continent, the wildflowers in Spring and Summer attract tourists almost as prolifically as they attract bees. The forests of the south-west are a symphony of colour and majesty in season, a fact borne out by the number of regions encompassed into national parks.

Denmark is situated on the shores of one of the delightful inlets that perforate the south coast of Western Australia. Wilson Inlet is larger than most, and is fed by the Denmark and Hay rivers, creating a wide, open expanse of still water ideally suited both to water sports and to the profusion of wildfowl which are to be found at all times of the year. As a result, nature lovers can indulge their hobbies in the quieter reaches with camera or notepad, while sailors, water-skiers and canoeists can cleave the still surface of the inlet close to the population centres. The coastal

areas are, as mentioned, strikingly beautiful, with the fine ocean beaches only a couple of kilometres from the town centre.

The beaches are one of the main features of Denmark's popularity as a vacation spot. A good surf rolls in on the ocean beaches, but there is quiet water at the entrance to Wilson Inlet, so there is something to suit everyone. Likewise, sailboarders can skim across the still surface of the Inlet, or wave-jump on the surf off Ocean Beach. Small sailcraft and canoes are better confined to the Inlet for the open sea off Ocean Beach can be ferocious at times, and even surfing can be dangerous, especially on the small beaches near Wilson Head. The quaintly named Madfish Bay is just to the west and the beautiful William Bay National Park, with its crystal-clear rock pools is also within easy reach.

Next to the ocean beaches, the

Inlet is the popular holiday spot, for its still waters make for good fishing as well as for the various water sports mentioned earlier. Trailer-sailers can enjoy this Inlet, for there are reasonable launching facilities for most sizes of craft, and the water, albeit shallow in places, is well-suited to the light-drafted trailer boats. One of the really nice things to do on Wilson Inlet, is to sail into the far reaches, then just drift quietly near the shore, watching the wide variety of bird life that inhabits this waterway. Cormorants, sandpipers, black swans and wild duck are but a few of the many species to be watched and photographed in their natural habitat.

The township of Denmark is neat and attractive, set, as it is, on a rise overlooking the river. There is accommodation in motels and guest houses with caravan parks at points around the inlet.

The coast in the vicinity of Denmark is dramatic and rugged

COSY CORNER

I am always suspicious of places called 'Cosy Corner'. For one thing there are too many of them, and for another the term is too trite, seeming to indicate that this is the only cosy corner on the coast. However, in the case of the Cosy Corner that lies on the southern coast of Western Australia, the name is most appropriate. The little settlement, which consists of a small camping ground and a motel, is tucked into the southern corner of Torbay Bay, snug and protected against bad weather and the aggressive Southern Ocean.

It is cosy, it is picturesque and it is ideal for family holidays. Torbay Head protrudes well out from the coast to create a perfect backwater for the big swells that sweep up from the south-west. Farther round Torbay Bay these swells make good surf, but in Cosy Corner they are broken down to a moderate size and a gaggle of rocks in the near vicinity reduces the waves to a quite acceptable size for young children and those who prefer relatively quiet water swimming. Like so many of the beaches along the south coast,

By road	430km SE of Perth
RAC Depot	See Albany
Caravan access	Sealed road all the way
Best weather	November thru' March
Accommodation	1 motel, 1 caravan park
Beaches	Cosy Corner Beach
Rock fishing	Excellent
Beach fishing	Excellent
Offshore fishing	Excellent, but launching may be difficult
Still water fishing	Limited
Sailing	Limited, open sea only
Sailboarding	Good, open sea only
Trailer-sailers	Not suitable
Water skiing	Limited, open sea only
Canoeing	Limited, open sea only
Skindiving	Excellent
Fuel and Bait	See Albany
Boat hire	None
Ramps	Over-beach only
National Parks	None
Interests	Attractive coast and hinterland

Torbay Bay offers a choice of surf or quiet water.

The same quiet water makes for easy boat launching, although once again, launching anything other than small boats is inhibited by ramp conditions. Boats must be launched over the beach in Cosy Corner and this means a four-wheel drive vehicle for anything carried on a trailer. This is a pity because offshore fishing grounds are prolific but access to them depends on whether or not you possess a four-wheel drive vehicle. The state of the sea and weather conditions will also play a part, of course, but in this well-sheltered spot such conditions are not as great a factor as they are on more exposed ramps.

Fishing from the beach or the rocks is easy and rewarding, if what the locals say is true. Certainly there is access to both, but there is no still-water fishing in the area. Skindiving is well-suited to these clear, unpolluted waters, as it is along the whole of this coastline, and sailing would be easy for catamarans and small boats, although they should not venture

too far out into Torbay Bay as the headland only protects the end of the Bay, and beyond that it is open ocean. Sailboards will have a field day either skipping out from Cosy Corner or wave-jumping farther down the beach.

Accomodation at Cosy Corner is different, to say the least. The motel is set well back from the beach, entailing quite a walk to

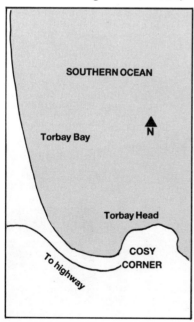

A cosy corner of Cosy Corner!

reach the surf, and even farther to get into Cosy Corner itself. The camping ground, which is set right into the corner, right on the beach, is not available for camping between December and March. I am sure there is a good reason for this, presumably the area is kept clear for day visitors from Albany. At all events, that is what the sign says, so if you are thinking of staying over at Cosy Corner during the summer months, you had better contact Albany Shire Council!

Outside beach and water activities, there is not much to offer at Cosy Corner. Walking across Torbay Head and West Cape Howe will provide an interesting exercise and reveal the magnificent coastline that forms the southern bastion of Western Australia. The relentless pounding of the Southern Ocean, surging up from the Antarctic, has carved this coastline into dramatic but exhilarating sculptures. Any stretch between Cape Leeuwin and King Georges Sound is a natural masterpiece with dimensions and character quite unique to this part of the world.

ALBANY

The story of Albany is the story of whaling. Although there is, of course, much more to this major southern port than just whaling, Albany's origins lie in whaling, its history is steeped in whaling, and on present indications, whaling is going to play a big part in Albany's future.

Fortunately the future will be less gruesome than the past and the innocent giants of the Southern Ocean who have suffered so cruelly at the hand of man for centuries will not be required to suffer any more. The future interest in whaling will be in the history and tradition of that industry and the sea-going mammals around whom the whole thing revolved. The old whaling station at Albany has been con-verted into a magnificent whaling museum where the full story of the industry, the men, the ships and the mammals is retold in one of the finest exhibits in the world.

No inlet around the south-west coast of Australia is more suited to maritime activities than King George Sound. At one time it was called the 'naval key to the eastern colonies' because of its strategic position and fine enclosed water in which a whole battle fleet could anchor with ease. During World War 1 it was the assembly point for the Australian fleet transporting the AIF to the Middle East war zone. In World War 2 it was an important US naval base.

It was the fine harbour and its strategic position that caused its early settlement. A party of convicts and troops were sent to establish a base there in 1826 at a time when fears were held that the French, who had been active in the area, might attempt to colonise the western side of the continent. The British, realising the value of King George Sound as a military outpost, established a garrison on the shores of the Sound.

The garrison was later transferred to Fremantle, but the fine harbour and small township of Albany remained to achieve even greater heights as the development centre of the south-west region of the continent. At one time King George Sound was the only port-of-call in Western Australia for mail steamers, and was also a major

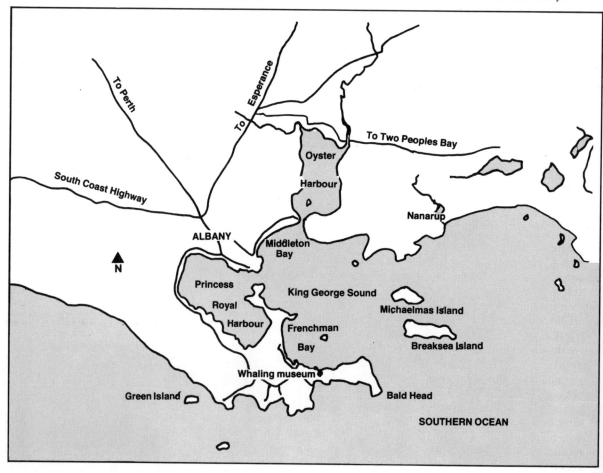

The old whaling station tucked under the massive bulk of Bald Head

coaling station. Its inner waterway of Princess Royal Harbour became the principal outlet for produce from the rich hinterland, a role which it plays to this day. And the whaling station at Frenchman Bay became the last shore-based whaling station in the Southern Hemisphere before its closure in 1978.

Such a magnificent harbour, set among some of Australia's most spectacular coastal scenery, creates interest from a far wider circle than just the maritime industry. Historically it is significant because it is the site of the first white settlement in Western Australia. Scenically it is important for the south-west coastal region is fast becoming the major tourist attraction of the State. Albany, on the shores of King George Sound, is the focal point of all tourist activities in the area. History is alive in the little township

where the buildings along the waterfront have changed little with the passing years. New developments in the town centre have been carefully controlled, so that while it is a modern town, well-equipped for an influx of visitors, it retains its old facade and the nostalgic atmosphere of days long past.

The town is attractively built on the hillside overlooking Princess Royal Harbour—a classic settlement in a classic setting. It is not hard to visualise long queues of horse and bullock teams waiting patiently for their turn to unload at the wharves. The wharves themselves have changed little since the tall masts of windjammers reared high above the sheds and long, thin funnels belched black smoke out over the bay. Nor is it hard to picture the drays and buggies making their way down the wide main

By Road 413km SE of Perth
RAC Depot 108 Albany Highway, Phone 41 1333
Caravan access Sealed highway
Best weather November thru' February
Accommodation 11 caravan parks, 8 motels, 4 hotels, 3 hotel/motels, 9 guest houses.
Beaches Goode Beach. Ledge Beach. Middleton Beach
Rock fishing Excellent
Beach fishing Excellent
Offshore fishing Excellent
Still water fishing Good in inlets and bays
Sailing Excellent
Sailboarding Excellent
Trailer-sailers Excellent
Water skiing Excellent
Canoeing Excellent
Skindiving Excellent on offshore islands and reefs
Fuel and Bait Town stores
Boat hire Emu Point
Ramps Emu Point. Town jetty. Frenchman Bay
National Parks Torndirrup N P
Interests Whaleworld. Frenchman Bay. Superb coastal scenery in Torndirrup N P. Old buildings in township

street, their horses braced back against the harness straps to counter the steep incline. Nostalgia is heavy in Albany, and it is one of this delightful town's most attractive features.

Matching the appeal of the town is the surrounding countryside with its geographical splendour. The harbour is deeply etched into a coastline of grey, bald granite hills, some of which rear up like surfacing whales close to the town itself. The bald granite, worn smooth by centuries of weathering, is a feature of this coast, from Cape Leeuwin, the south-western tip of the continent, to Cape Le Grand at the edge of the Great Australian Bight. It makes striking visual spectacles both inland, where huge monoliths rear up for hundreds of metres out of bushland, and along the coastline where it allows the sea to flood in between giant outcrops, creating superb sheltered waterways such as King George Sound. Some outcrops emerge from the sea as islands, equally bald and equally striking. In the vicinity of the entrance to King George Sound there are no less than nine such islands, creating not only a visual impact, but also a very practical breakwater against the big rollers of the Southern Ocean.

Being the only major harbour in the south-west region, Albany is much used by both pleasure and commercial vessels

Such scenic magnficence must be preserved for all time, and the coastal region to the south and west of Albany is covered by one of Western Australia's most unique national parks. The Tondirrup National Park, although not large by comparison with some national parks along the southern coastline, contains a wealth of interest. Geographical, geological, historical and botanical features abound in this Park, ranging from the striking natural rock formations of the coast to the restored and refurbished whaling museum at Frenchman Bay.

This unique project offers an insight into the adventurous days when men in small rowboats pitted their skill against the giant whales of the Southern Ocean, and contains a fine collection of relics of whaling days down the ages, including a real-life modern 600 tonne whalechaser, complete with the explosive harpoon equipment which decimated the whales almost to the point of extinction.

To attempt to detail all of Albany's attractions would be to write a book on that town alone. Sufficient to say that this delightful town on the shores of one of Australia's finest harbours must rate a priority on any traveller's itinerary. It is not enough simply to visit Albany, for there is as much of interest outside the town as there is in the old buildings and the extensive waterway. To see all that this southern town has to offer would require at least a couple of weeks, and that would cover only sightseeing. If you plan to enjoy the beaches in the area, fish the prolific harbour or the offshore reefs, sail the extensive waters of King George Sound or sun and swim at one of the neighbouring coastal havens, then you had better spend more than one holiday in this wonderful south coast town.

NANARUP

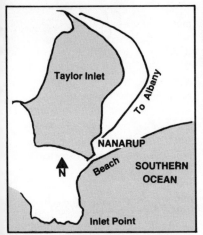

Paperbarks line the inlet at Nanarup

On first acquaintances it is a little hard to take Nanarup seriously, for a sign at the parking area states, in effect that when the water temperature exceeds 24 degrees celsius, the water may contain an amoeba which causes potentially fatal amoebic meningitis. This is quite a notice to find on the foreshores of the beach you have chosen for a day's outing with the kiddies, but there it is as large as life.

Happily the waters referred to are the waters of the inlet locked behind the sandbar and it does not refer to the sparkling clear ocean beyond the bar. Nevertheless it is an alarming notice for parents in particular to read, and the authorities are to be commended for drawing such immediate attention in such a dramatic way.

A little farther on there is another notice which advises that vehicles must not turn right beyond this notice. Since immediately beyond the sign is water, this notice is perhaps not meant to be taken quite so seriously. The fact is, of course, that over-sand vehicles must be regulated like any other vehicles. It is just the location of the sign that makes it hard to take seriously.

There are no more dramatic or humorous signs in Nanarup that I can recall. This is a small, not very tidy village with no stores and no

caravan park. Indeed, all it has to offer is its beach, but that is magnificent and makes up for the lack of other amenities. A wide, sweeping surf beach backed by high dunes, it is extremely popular with surfers, swimmers and fishermen. It also has quiet water for children—not in the inlet, of course, but in the western corner of the bay where the swell is broken.

This is a good spot to launch a boat, but as with all the beaches along this coast, you will need a tractor or a four-wheel drive vehicle to do so. This is more so the case with Nanarup than most beaches because there is not even an access way through the dunes and boats must be towed along the edge of the inlet and across the sand bar. Launching small boats would be easier, but they still have to be brought from the car park. Perhaps floating them down the inlet might be the answer. I would suspect that all this is really too much trouble and the only boats brought in and launched are those of locals or regulars who know the ropes.

Nanarup Beach is well worth a visit, just for the day, even if you do nothing but relax on the beach. There are pleasant walks over the high sandhills, all of which reveal superb panoramas of the bay and

the coastline. Wildflowers grow in profusion there during the spring and summer and kids will love the scramble through the scrub and sea grass. There is a rocky headland at the western end of the beach for rock fishermen and the water is crystal clear, inviting skindivers to enjoy the underwater scenery.

There are questionable toilets at the car park but that is the sum total of amenities at Nanarup. It is essentially a spot for day visiting, since it is so close to Albany. That is probably why it has not developed more and better facilities.

By road 435km SE of Perth
RAC Depot See Albany
Caravan access Sealed road all the way
Best weather November thru' February
Accommodation None (limited camping)
Beaches Nanarup Beach
Rock fishing Good
Beach fishing Excellent
Offshore fishing Excellent, but launching difficult
Still water fishing Fair in Inlet
Sailing Good in Inlet
Sailboarding Excellent, Inlet or open sea
Trailer-sailers Limited in Inlet
Water skiing Excellent in Inlet
Canoeing Excellent in Inlet
Skindiving Excellent on offshore reefs
Fuel and Bait See Albany
Boat hire None
Ramps Over-beach only
National Parks None
Interests Wildlife in Inlet

TWO PEOPLES BAY

Two Peoples Bay is a nature reserve with a ranger's office the only building, and the entire area inhabited solely by wildlife. The main beach is the whitest of white sand and sweeps away from the picnic area in the western corner, right around the bay to the east where it terminates at the foot of a huge, often cloud-capped mountain. Dramatic is the only appropriate description of the coastline on either side of Two Peoples Bay, for behind the western corner, high hills studded with giant granite rocks also reach up to the clouds.

In that corner, beneath the coastal hills, the beach is tucked hard up under the headland and therefore very sheltered. A reef off the tip of the headlands breaks the swell down to a little more than a ripple so it is an ideal spot for quiet-water swimming and boat launching. The former is well-suited for young families and the latter for those who like their sport out on the open sea.

However, the ramp is only an access ramp to the beach and launching a boat from a trailer will require a four-wheel drive vehicle. Small boats which can be dragged across the sand will have no trouble, so centreboarders, catamarans and canoes will have a field-day here. Sailboards, of course, can launch anywhere, and surf riders will need to carry their boards farther round the bay if they want to ride big waves.

Fishing is excellent in whatever form it comes. The granite headlands provide good platforms for rock-hoppers while the beach can be fished anywhere. Offshore fishermen will have to resolve the problem of getting their boat in the water, as will skindivers unless they plan to dive just round the headlands.

There is no accommodation at Two Peoples Bay. Being a nature

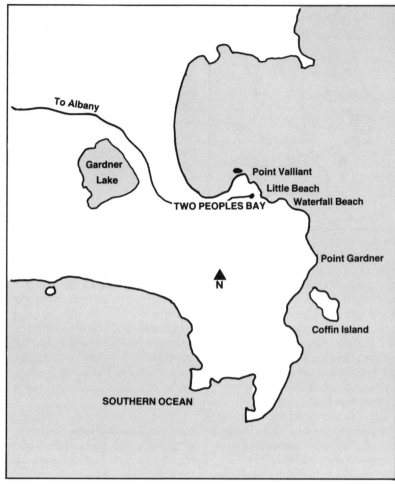

reserve, even camping is not permitted, so this is a spot to visit only on a day trip out from Albany. As such it makes an excellent venture because the drive in, although along a gravel road, is through delightful rolling countryside, green and lush and offset by the backdrop of big granite hills. Where the farmlands give way to the nature reserve, the bush is interesting and there is a small lake which is a fine haunt for wildfowl.

The main beach is called Waterfall Beach. Over the rise and tucked under the mountains is the startlingly beautiful Little Beach. This is purely for surfers because big rollers run in right onto the small beach. It is one of the most picturesque

By road	444km SE of Perth
RAC Depot	See Albany
Caravan access	Moderate gravel road from turnoff (14km)
Best weather	November thru' February
Accommodation	None (limited camping)
Beaches	Two Peoples Bay Beach
Rock fishing	Excellent
Beach fishing	Excellent
Offshore fishing	Excellent, but launching difficult
Still water fishing	None
Sailing	Limited, open sea only
Sailboarding	Limited, open sea only
Trailer-sailers	Not suitable
Water skiing	Limited, open sea only
Canoeing	Limited, open sea only
Skindiving	Excellent
Fuel and Bait	See Albany
Boat hire	None
Ramps	Over-beach only
National Parks	None
Interests	Magnificent coastal scenery

beaches in this area, indented right into the huge giant granite slopes of the towering coastal hills. However, it is very much a visual delight and not to be sampled unless you are a very experienced and strong swimmer.

If the water does not tempt you, Two Peoples Bay has quite a few other interests. Climbing the coastal hills would be tough but very rewarding for the coastal scenery in this area is quite splendid. Similarly, bush walkers will find a lot of interest in the nature reserve which, of course, is also a wildlife sanctuary. Farther back along the road is a completely contrasting attraction—a Marron farm. There may seem to be very little in Two Peoples Bay, but when you take a trip there, you will find that in fact there is something for almost every taste.

Typical south coast scenery at Two Peoples Bay

CHEYNE BEACH

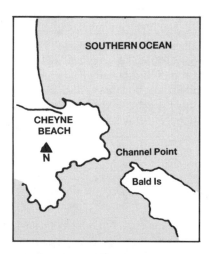

As you travel along the superb new road into Cheyne Beach, you will notice a game reserve on the left-hand side. Do not expect to see wild deer or any game of that nature, for this game reserve is to protect wildfowl which frequent the small, shallow lake nearby. On either side of the road the low coastal scrub makes an ideal location for a wide variety of wildflowers during spring and summer, not least of which is the striking red kangaroo paw.

Beyond the roadside scrub, the land has been cleared and low, undulating farmlands stretch right out to the coast where they terminate in magnificent boulder-studded granite hills. It is a delightfully scenic drive in and makes the trip worthwhile even before you reach the beach.

Unfortunately the settlement at Cheyne Beach does not live up to the promise of the drive in, for the few fishermen's cottages that are located on the bay are nondescript and do nothing to enhance the natural beauty. However, the foreshores are pleasant and the caravan park is nicely located away from the beach so it is unobtrusive while being practical. It is a well-planned park and does not detract from the attractiveness of the bush and the beach.

The beach is superb. A long, wide, white-sand beach sweeping round the perimeter of the bay to high hills on the eastern shore. The main body of the beach is called Hassell Beach, but to most the whole sandy strip is known as Cheyne Beach. From the quiet spot under Lookout Point at one end, to the steep granite cliffs at the other, this beach offers something for everyone, whether you take your sport quietly or prefer the excitement of big waves. The southern corner near the picnic area is ideal for youngsters because the big seas are broken by the headland and by Bald Island, and run onto the beach as quiet water. Across the main sweep of the beach there is surf—big surf. You can take your pick.

The launching ramp is similar to most others in the region, just an access to the sand and from then on launching must be by four-wheel drive vehicle. This obviously inhibits the use of the beach by many fishermen and other boat owners who tow their craft with a conventional car. Many of these bays would make good cruising

The rugged coastline near Cheyne Beach

By road	475km SE of Perth
RAC Depot	See Albany
Caravan access	Sealed road all the way
Best weather	November thru' February
Accommodation	Camping only
Beaches	Cheyne Beach. Hassell Beach
Rock fishing	Excellent
Beach fishing	Excellent
Offshore fishing	Excellent, but launching may be difficult
Still water fishing	None
Sailing	Limited, open sea only
Sailboarding	Good, open sea only
Trailer-sailers	Not suitable
Water skiing	Not suitable
Canoeing	Limited, open sea only
Skindiving	Excellent
Fuel and Bait	Highway service station
Boat hire	None
Ramps	Over-beach only
National Parks	None
Interests	Superb coastal scenery

grounds for trailer-sailers, but launching would be impossible over the sand.

Despite this, a number of boats put out from Cheyne Beach and the fishing offshore more than rewards the effort of getting the boat into the water. Rock-hoppers will find a number of spots around Lookout

Point where they can try their luck, while beach fishermen have the whole crescent of white sand from which to cast their rigs. Skindivers, too, are well catered-for since the water is brilliantly clear and there is interesting diving around the rocks and headlands. To dive off Bald Island would be doubly interesting, but getting a sizeable boat with all the scuba gear into the water could be a problem.

An interesting challenge would be to climb the range of coastal hills. The views from the top must be breathtaking. These particular hills are not as high as those to the westward, so even persons who are not too fit could make it. Not far along these hills is a small beach called Bettys Beach. It has no facilities and the beach itself is modest, but the coastal views as you drive down to it are superb. Well worth the drive down from the highway for a quick visit on the way to Cheyne Beach.

CAPE RICHE

There is no settlement at Cape Riche. A few scattered buildings in the bush is the only sign of habitation. The area popular with holiday makers is close up under the lee of two hills, one of which rejoices in the unlikely name of Mount Belcher. One assumes that it must have been at one time part of the volcano system and belched lava and smoke. Whatever the origins of the name, this mountain, together with Mount George, makes up the pointed headland called Cape Riche.

A small waterway runs out at the foot of these hills, creating Cheyne Inlet, an ideal shelter for ships caught out in the bad westerly or southerly weather. A small headland divides it from the main beach where the effects of any bad weather are even further minimised. Just offshore, Cheyne Island adds its bulk to the breakwater effect, so that by the time the waves reach the beach by the picnic area, they are but a ripple.

This is a common scene along the south coast of Western Australia. A small, tranquil corner of a bay,

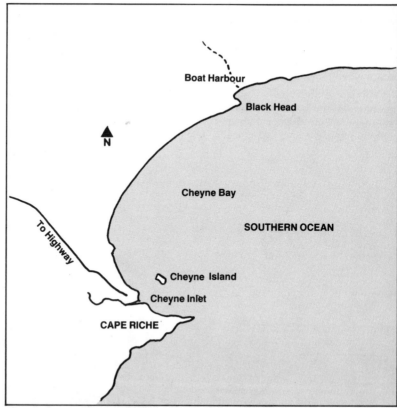

By road   525km SE of Perth
RAC Depot   See Albany
Caravan access   Good gravel road from highway turnoff
Best weather   November thru' February
Accommodation   Camping only
Beaches   Cheyne Bay Beach. Cape Riche Beach
Rock fishing   Excellent
Beach fishing   Excellent
Offshore fishing   Excellent, but launching may be difficult
Still water fishing   Limited, in Eyre River
Sailing   Limited, open sea only
Sailboarding   Good, open sea only
Trailer-sailers   Not suitable
Water skiing   Not suitable
Canoeing   Limited, open sea only
Skindiving   Excellent
Fuel and Bait   Highway service station (Wellstead)
Boat hire   None
Ramps   Over-beach only
National Parks   None
Interests   Superb coastal scenery

almost always the western corner, is utilised for holidaying and boat launching. And just as with other bays in this area, the boat launching ramp runs over the beach, thus involving the use of four-wheel drive vehicles for launching from trailers. It would seem that Western Australian boat owners must have the highest percentage of four-wheel drive vehicles per head of population otherwise they would never get their boats in the water!

For holidaying families this little corner is ideal. The water is quiet for the toddlers yet farther round there is surf for the 'oldies'. Board-riding and wave-jumping would be exhilarating, for the beach is shallow and the waves form well out. Often small craft such as catamarans, centreboarders and canoes can launch here and sail quite safely in the corner. Once out into the open bay , of course, conditions are

more severe, for this is a rugged coastline and sea and swell can be very ferocious when the wind gets up.

There is a camping ground right on the beach which is run by the shire, and to the best of my knowledge is unattended. But my survey was done in spring, so perhaps a ranger is located there during the peak summer season. It is an isolated spot for even at the highway junction there is only a small store, and the nearest town is about 80 kilometres away. So if you go in to stay, take everything with you. The store at Wellstead will take care of everyday needs but it is a long hike into town if you forget something important.

The area behind Cheyne Bay is mostly coastal scrub with some wheat land closer to the highway. There are good coastal walks but the going may get tough for this is virgin bushland and the only tracks will be those made by walkers before you. The road is gravel but in good condition so access is easy. Since there may be wildlife on the road drive carefully, especially at night, for this is real country and wildlife are not used to strangers.

A little farther along the coast are two spots popular with fishermen. One is called Boat Harbour and the other Pallinup Beach. Both are delightful spots, particularly Pallinup Beach which has much the same configuration as Cape Riche but with a longer river estuary.

There is a picnic area here but access is really restricted to four-wheel drive vehicles as it is to Boat Harbour. Since this guide is intended for vacationers with conventional vehicles, there is little point in giving these points more than a passing mention.

The surf is well broken beneath the lee of Cape Riche

BREMER BAY

Bremer Bay is a small, neat, but fairly uninteresting settlement a long way from the main population centres. This would seem to be a good reason not to take the long haul out, but there are a number of good reasons why you should. The most important of these is the huge Fitzgerald River National Park, which stretches from Bremer Bay to Hopetoun and covers a magnificent stretch of coast with a number of unique features. Although access for four-wheel drive vehicles is possible at a number of places, conventional vehicles can only get to the Park through Hopetoun and Bremer Bay.

Other good reasons to visit Bremer Bay revolve almost entirely around the water. The fishing is excellent, sailing in any form is first-class, skindiving is superb and the beaches are unending. From a family holiday point of view this would seem to encompass everything, but there is also bushwalking, delightful coastal scenery and wildflowers in profusion. It is certainly a fairly isolated spot, but then many people, myself included, prefer holidays away from the madding crowds, and with 242,739 hectares of national park on your doorstep you cannot get much more isolated than that!

The problem in describing the Fitzgerald River National Park is where to begin. A wide diversity of geological, geographical and botanical features are encompassed within its boundaries, covering one of the loveliest stretches of the south coast. Originally an undulating sand plain, the area has been eroded by high rainfall rivers such as the Fitzgerald, the Gairdner, the Hamersley and the Phillips. Wide, flat valleys filled with dense scrub have been carved in the sand plain along the courses of these rivers, contrasting sharply with the open heathlands that lie between them. In places the erosion of the watercourses has gouged deep gorges or created colourful spongolite cliffs.

The geology of the coast is similarly varied, with the eastern coastline forming spectacular cliffs against which the fury of the Southern Ocean crashes in a constant welter of white foam. In complete contrast, the western half of the coastal strip is composed mainly of long, unbroken beaches where the same ocean rollers come ashore as heavy surf. Access to these beaches is for the most part confined to four-wheel drive vehicles although Tooregullup Beach, at the southern end, has a passable gravel road most of the way. There is a choice here of still-water fishing in Gordon Inlet,

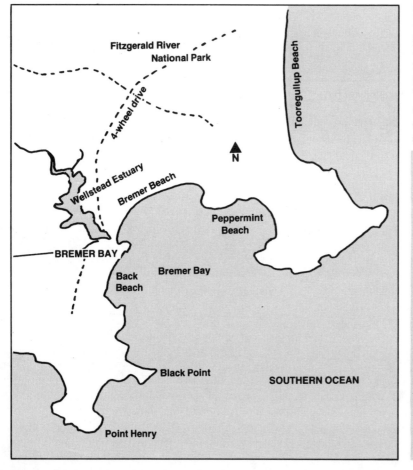

By road 507km SE of Perth
RAC Depot See Albany
Caravan access Sealed road all the way
Best weather November thru' February
Accommodation 1 caravan park
Beaches Dillon Beach. Bremer Beach. Back Beach
Rock fishing Excellent
Beach fishing Excellent
Offshore fishing Excellent, but launching may be difficult
Still water fishing Good in Wellstead Estuary
Sailing Good
Sailboarding Excellent
Trailer-sailers Launching too difficult
Water skiing Good, but launching may be difficult
Canoeing Excellent in Bremer River
Skindiving Excellent on headlands and offshore reefs
Fuel and Bait Local store
Boat hire None
Ramps Over-beach only
National Parks Fitzgerald River NP
Interests Superb coastal scenery

Crystal clear water and good fishing are features of Bremer Bay

or ocean beach fishing on the interminable stretch of beach running north from Whalebone Point.

In the immediate vicinity of Bremer Bay there is a similar choice of fishing and swimming. Wellstead Estuary is renown for its Bream, while the beaches to the north and south of the town face directly out to sea and therefore offer first-class surf fishing. Boats can be launched into the estuary over the foreshores and there is an over-beach ramp in the corner of John Cove, the southern-most indentation of Bremer Bay. Launching on this ramp may be difficult with a conventional vehicle and sea conditions, although usually quiet in this corner, can also affect launching. Sailboards and small sailboats can usually sail off the beach, although conditions can get rough in the open bay. The still water of the Inlet is, of course, ideal for all boating.

Rock fishing is possible from a number of headlands, the closest to the town being just to the south of Back Beach, while fishermen with a four-wheel drive vehicle will have an enormous choice of both headlands and beaches all around the district. Access to Dillon Bay is by gravel road as far as the homestead, the remaining distance to the beach is limited to four-wheel drive vehicles. Indeed, it would be safe to say that with the exception of Bremer Beach and the beaches in the immediate vicinity of the town, access to most areas both near Bremer Bay and in the Fitgerald River National Park are limited to four-wheel drive vehicles only.

Accommodation is in the form of a caravan park and a camping ground, while there are camping facilities in the National Park. There are a couple of stores in the town and another at the highway junction at Wellstead. Other than that, facilities are somewhat limited, for as mentioned earlier, this is an area where holidays are enjoyed close to nature, and the trappings of city living are left far behind.

HOPETOUN

Whaling is Australia's oldest industry. Long before settlers came to till the land whalers of all nationalities used the more sheltered bays and inlets for their gruesome trade. Many of the ships which brought convicts to this land were converted to whalers when they had unloaded their human cargoes. They then set forth to capture and kill the mammals which would provide their return cargoes. The small indented bays around the coastline were ideal bases from which to operate, and since the whales were particularly prolific in southern waters, many southern bays supported a whaling industry or provided a haven for the ships.

Mary Anne Harbour, some 350 kilometres by road to the east of Albany, was just such a bay. The waters of the Southern Ocean have always been closely linked to whaling and a major whaling industry flourished along the south-western coast of Australia until as recently as 1978, when the last whaling company ceased operating from Frenchman Bay, Albany. In the early 1800s, bays such as Mary

Anne Harbour rang to the roistering of whaling crews pursuing their arduous calling among the delightful scenery of the south-west coast. When they departed, the bays returned to their former peaceful state until settlers brought their flocks to the inland regions and used the harbours as havens for loading and unloading their boats.

This was the scene for many years at Mary Anne Harbour. Then the discovery of copper and gold at Ravensthorpe, 50 kilometres inland, changed the little harbour into an important port. With virtually no other means of getting the precious minerals to their markets, the small bay on the south coast was developed into a port with a jetty capable of accommodating quite sizeable ships and with a railway link to inland Ravensthorpe. The town which sprang up around the port was named Hopetoun and once again the quiet coastal bay became a hive of bustling activity. Those days are long since gone and now fishermen create the only action along the waterfront. The jetty is still there, but the ships no longer call

and the railway closed in 1936. Produce from the rural hinterland is mostly taken by road to distant centres such as Albany or Perth.

But the little port of Hopetoun is enjoying a new boom, as are all the settlements along this coastline. Tourists have discovered the lovely beaches and striking coastal scenery around the town, as well as the Fitzgerald River National Park, which contains the superb Barren Ranges. Hopetoun lies at the eastern extremity of this Park and provides access along Hamersley Drive past Culham Inlet to some of the Park's most striking scenery. Four Mile Beach, Barrens Beach Mylies Beach and West Beach can all be reached after only a few minutes drive along this road, while Hamersley Inlet can also be reached by four-wheel drive vehicles or on foot. This superb national park must form the highlight of any visit to Hopetoun.

Other activities revolve mostly around the water. Swimming, fishing and sailing are all popular, as is skindiving, for the water is crystal clear and the rocky headlands

By road   584km S of Perth
RAC Depot   See Ravensthorpe, AJ and MA King, Phone 38 1146, 38 1056
Caravan access   Sealed road all the way
Best weather   November thru' February
Accommodation   1 caravan park, 1 hotel
Beaches   Superb coastal beaches
Rock fishing   Excellent
Beach fishing   Excellent
Offshore fishing   Excellent, but launching may be difficult
Still water fishing   Good from jetty
Sailing   Good, open sea only
Sailboarding   Excellent
Trailer-sailers   Launching too difficult
Water skiing   Limited
Canoeing   Good, open sea only
Skindiving   Excellent
Fuel and Bait   Local store
Boat hire   None
Ramps   Over-beach only
National Parks   Fitzgerald River N P
Interests   Superb coastal scenery. Historic old buildings

Four-wheel drive is essential for launching on most parts of this coastline

contain a great number of interesting underwater features. Culham Inlet is a landlocked stretch of water alive with wildlife of every kind, in particular wildfowl. Coastal walks in this area are very rewarding and photographers will have their cameras clicking constantly, so magnificent is the scenery and so varied the features. The land-based side of holiday activities will be related mostly to walking and sight-seeing, for there is not much in the way of organised sport. But with access to such superb natural features, who needs man-made activities.

Hopetoun is 50 kilometres from Ravensthorpe and the main highway, and since this whole region is fairly thinly populated, a visit would necessarily involve a stay. There is a caravan park and an historic old hotel and a few shops with the necessities of life. Camping is permitted in the Fitzgerald River National Park and advice can be obtained from the Ranger at the Hamersley Drive entrance. For a different, away-from-it-all type of holiday, Hopetoun is the place. If you are just passing, make a point of taking a run down the access road to the town, for it will reveal some of the finest scenery you will see along this coastline.

ESPERANCE

Like Ceduna, its counterpart on the opposite side of the Nullabor Plains, Esperance lies on the fringe of the massive wheat belts that mark the end of rural development and signal the beginning of the desert conditions which dominate the whole of the central Australian region. From the Kimberleys in the north to the Great Australian Bight in the south, the whole of the continental land mass is a conglomeration of harsh, arid country, spinifex plains and desert. This belt divides the country geographically into two entirely seperate habitable regions with only scattered settlements in between.

Three great deserts comprise most of this arid belt; the Gibson, Great Sandy and Great Victorian deserts. These are interspersed with salt lakes and tortured ranges, a geographical scenario which does not permit the encroachment of any rural development other than limited grazing. On the fringe of these deserts, the modern pioneer settlers live the hardship that their forefathers endured as they coax the dusty, unproductive soil to support a struggling crop. Some are winning the battle. Hundreds of thousands of hectares of this flat, featureless land has been cultivated to produce grain harvests, and regions such as the western fringes of the central deserts are now slowly being converted into massive grain fields.

Before rail and road became the major medium for transporting this grain, isolated bays and harbours along the coastline were developed into ports from which the harvests could be exported. Just such a port is Esperance, located on the south-western coastline of the continent, on the edge of the wasteland that is the Nullabor Plain. Because of the development of huge tracts of land to the north and west, Esperance has become a major shipping outlet and one of Western Australia's major ports for the export of grain, sheep and wool. The harbour is dominated by a huge silo, as are so many of these grain shipping ports, and giant road trains, loaded with hundreds of sheep, thunder into the town from the distant stations of the inland.

But if primary industry is Esperance's main concern, a fast developing secondary industry is claiming a great deal of attention. This is tourism, for the scenic delights of the coastal regions around the port are attracting more and more visitors every year. Similarly, its location close to the commencement of the Eyre Highway, makes Esperance a natural stopover for visitors from the east who have just completed the dusty crossing of the Nullabor. What could be more refreshing after a 1500 kilometre haul across the desert from Ceduna than the magnificent coastal scenery around Esperance. High, bald granite rocks sweeping down through coastal scrub into small bays with brilliantly clear blue water and clean, sandy

By road   725km SE of Perth
RAC Depot   Ocean Motors Pty Ltd, Phone 71 1216, 71 1228
Caravan access   Sealed road all the way
Best weather   November thru' February
Accommodation   7 caravan parks, 4 motels, 2 hotels, 1 hotel/motel
Beaches   Twilight Cove. Town beach. Coastal beaches
Rock fishing   Excellent
Beach fishing   Excellent
Offshore fishing   Excellent
Still water fishing   Good in harbour
Sailing   Excellent
Sailboarding   Excellent
Trailer-sailers   Good, launching relatively easy
Water skiing   Excellent
Canoeing   Excellent
Skindiving   Excellent
Fuel and Bait   Town stores
Boat hire   None
Ramps   Good. In harbour
National Parks   Cape Le Grand N P
Interests   Historic buildings. Busy Port. Superb coastal scenery in Cape Le Grand National Park

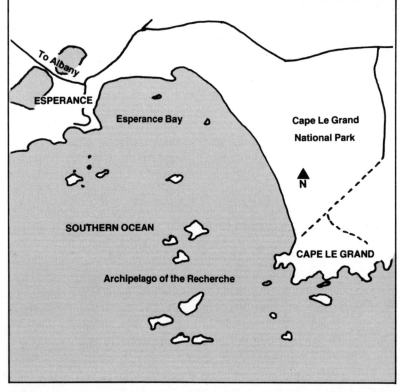

crescents of beach forms the scenery along much of the coast here. Tall sand dunes with never-ending beaches are to be found along the remainder.

There is so much to see and do in Esperance that visitors tend to stay much longer than planned. There is not much in the way of man-made attractions, but the natural features are in many cases breathtaking. So much so that large sections of the adjacent coastline are protected as fine national parks. Cape Le Grand and Cape Arid national parks lie to the east of the town while to the west is the smaller but delightful Stokes National Park and the huge Fitzgerald River National Park. Such a proliferation of national parks along such a relatively short section of coastline says much for the natural beauty of this region.

Cape Le Grand National Park is

only about 45 minutes drive from Esperance along good roads. It is a very spectacular park with granite headlands and outcrops forming bays and inlets fringed with white sand. There is a proliferation of wildlife both in the clear blue water and in the coastal scrub that covers the coastline but is broken frequently by protrusions of smooth, round granite rocks and hills. It is a paradise for those who like to get far away from civilisation and enjoy nature in its total isolation. The offshore islands of the Recherche Archipelago create a magnificent seascape. Access to the islands is via Esperance harbour or Lucky Bay, in the heart of the Park, where there is a reasonable boat launching facility. Camping is allowed at Lucky Bay and Le Grand Beach.

The township of Esperance has a great deal for visiting holidaymak-

ers. The beaches along the town foreshore are pleasant and there are numerous nearby beaches of which Twilight Cove, with its silver sand and rocky islets, is the most popular. Historic homesteads are scattered around the area, the most interesting being the original home of the Dempster brothers, Esperance's first settlers. This house has been classified by the National Trust and its owners have restored it with great care to retain the atmosphere of those early times.

The headstone of Aboriginal Tommy Windich is preserved by the Esperance Bay Municipal Museum and is another link with the region's past. Tommy was a faithful tracker and companion of explorer John Forrest, whom he accompanied on four expeditions, two of which were from Adelaide to Perth. The inscription on the tombstone was written by Alexander and John Forrest.

A magnificent stretch of beach near Esperance

Bald rocky islands are a feature of the Recherche Archipelago

In such a region, pleasant sunny holidays are guaranteed. The beaches provide every form of swimming, from still water pools among the rocks to surf on the long, open beaches. Fishing for almost any species is possible since there are rocky headlands, sandy beaches, and good ramps on which to launch boats for offshore fishing. The islands of the offshore groups ensure that there is always plenty of fish in the area, and the seals and other wildlife which inhabit these islands are proof of this. Seals tend to congregate in areas where there is a wealth of their staple diet, and fishermen cannot go far wrong by fishing those same waters. There are jetties and charter boats to complete the fishing picture, so it follows that if you cannot catch a fish somewhere in the Esperance area, you are unlikely to catch one anywhere.

Sailing, sailboarding, canoeing and water-skiing are equally popular on the delightfully clear waters of the beaches and bays in the area. Perhaps one of the most popular water sports is skindiving, for the offshore islands and rocks make a perfect venue for fish and wildfowl of all kinds. You can dive among the seals, who seem to enjoy human company in their own element under the surface, often frolicking around divers like kids in the local swimming pool. Fairy penguins and other wildlife are also to be seen on these islands, even sometimes on the shore. If your diving is not up to this standard, then snorkelling among the rocks around the shore will provide almost as much interest, for the waters along this coastline are sparklingly clear and unpolluted.

It is a long haul out to Esperance from Albany or the other main centres of the west, so if you intend to visit, you will need to stay. The town is well organised for accommodation and the shopping centre caters for all needs. If you are planning to cross the Nullabor in either direction, put Esperance on your list as a must for an extended stopover on the way.

ISRAELITE BAY

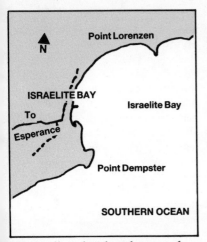

The striking Red Kangaroo-paw

The small, isolated settlement of Israelite Bay came into being as a result of the establishment of a telegraph line between the eastern and western States. The line ran via Eucla, at the head of the Great Australian Bight, to Albany. The cable was erected along the coast with great difficulty, for construction supplies could only come by sea as there was no road access. From Eucla westwards for some 200 kilometres, steep cliffs prevent boats landing almost anywhere and the construction of the line was held up until a solitary gap was found in the cliffs around 60 kilometres east of Point Culver. When the problems were finally overcome a station was opened at Israelite Bay on December 5 1876. The line was completed and the tiny settlement on the west side of the Bight became an important waypoint. Postal engineers and their families moved in and established the original town.

Nowadays Israelite Bay is a small, isolated settlement containing a number of historic features, the most important of which is the old Post Office, regrettably falling into ruins. In the countryside of the nearby Thomas River are other historic remains, mostly of homesteads of the pioneers that first established their sheep runs on the sparse pastoral leases. Despite its attractive coastline, Israelite Bay is too far from major population centres to attract a great deal of tourist traffic, but it is a popular fishing spot and many fishermen make the long haul out to this, the last settlement on the Western Australia coastline before the massive cliffs of the Great Australian Bight preclude launching a boat of any description.

There is no accommodation, although camping is permitted, and the local stores have limited but adequate supplies. There is boat access over a beach ramp to the prolific, but rugged offshore waters where diving is as good as the fishing. The 200 kilometre road out from Esperance is in good shape and provides an easy drive for conventional vehicles. It passes through the Cape Arid National Park close to towering Mount Baring. Israelite Bay is not a spot for a stopover, or even for a quick visit, as it is too far off the beaten track. Indeed, there is not a great deal to offer even for a prolonged visit unless you like your holidays in total isolation.

By road   924km SE of Perth
RAC Depot   See Esperance
Caravan access   Good road all the way
Best weather   November thru' February
Accommodation   1 caravan park
Beaches   Israelite Bay. Coastal beaches
Rock fishing   Good
Beach fishing   Excellent
Offshore fishing   Good, but launching may be difficult
Still water fishing   Limited
Sailing   Good, open sea only
Sailboarding   Excellent
Trailer-sailers   Launching too difficult
Water skiing   Launching difficult
Canoeing   Good, open sea only
Skindiving   Excellent
Fuel and Bait   Local store
Boat hire   None
Ramps   Over-beach only
National Parks   Cape Arid N P
Interests   Historic ruins. Magnificent coastal scenery

INDEX